A WISH TO BE

⁄is was born in Birkenhead in 1898, joined the
16 as a ⁄ilot and was awarded the MC. After
we⁊t to Peking to teach the Chinese to fly. All
.. ⁊ded in *Sagittarius Rising*, recognized as a
⁊orld War classic. Returning to London he be-
⁊ne of the five founding members of the BBC and
⁊an of the Programme Board from 1922 to 1926.
⁊nt on to write books and radio plays, directed the
⁊o films made of Bernard Shaw's plays, was called
⁊llywood where he got an Oscar for his script of
⁊lion, went on to beachcomb in Tahiti and re-
⁊ flying duties in the RAF in the Second World
⁊ 947 he flew his own aeroplane to South Africa
wi⁊ ⁊armed sheep. Returning to New York to work
for t⁊ ⁊ited Nations in 1951, he was subsequently
invited ⁊ ⁊ ⁊ staff⁊of Associated Rediffusion when
commercial television was set up in London a year later.
He retired to Corfu in 1968.

A Wish To Be

A VOYAGE OF DISCOVERY

Cecil Lewis

E L E M E N T
Shaftesbury, Dorset ● Rockport, Massachusetts
Brisbane, Queensland

© Cecil Lewis 1994

First published in Great Britain in 1994 by
Element Books Limited
Shaftesbury, Dorset

Published in the USA in 1994 by
Element, Inc.
42 Broadway, Rockport, MA 01966

Published in Australia by
Element Books Limited for
Jacaranda Wiley Limited,
33 Park Road, Milton, Brisbane, 4064

Cover illustration by Images Colour Library
Cover design by Bridgewater Books
Text design by Roger Lightfoot
Typeset by Footnote Graphics, Warminster, Wiltshire
Printed and bound in Great Britain by
Redwood Books Limited, Trowbridge, Wiltshire

British Library Cataloguing in Publication
data available

Library of Congress Cataloging in publication
data available

ISBN 1–85230–534–7

Contents

A Wish To Be

The short aphorisms that head this collection of reflections are all taken from the work of Gurdjieff.

ADVICE TO THE READER

A bit at a time.

FOREWORD

The Power of an Idea

'There is in our life a very great purpose and we must all
serve this Great Common Purpose. In this lies the whole
sense and predestination of our life.'

The late publication of this series of short morning talks
broadcast some years ago on the World Service of the
BBC confirms that a man's life may not be finished at the
standard retiring age of sixty-five and may indeed go on
maturing for years without loss of clarity. Looking back I
recognize the slow discovery (over thirty years) of the simplicity at the heart of our inner life.

The study of Gurdjieff's ideas* when I first met them fifty
years ago gave me a sense of framework and scale within
which to glimpse the whole structure of the universe, and my
own infinitesimal relation to it, as one majestic whole.

This attempt to try to understand the roots of how we all
live together and where we are going grew more and more
absorbing the more I studied it. Although it had been the
world's preoccupation for thousands of years and every great
religious teacher had, in different words, repeated the same
truths, it still remained the main obstacle to harmony in
human society.

In fact the Fall of Man begins here! From the earliest days
so-called 'wise men' began to hide, embroider and embellish

---

* *All and Everything* by G. I. Gurdjieff, an objectively impartial criticism of
the life of Man. Also *Beelzebub's Tales to His Grandson*.

A Wish To Be

this central need – to love and worship God – with every sort of fancy, legend, dream or fairy tale. Man, it seems, has a built-in disposition to kill the thing he loves.

However at least it seems the intelligence and insatiable curiosity of science has forced these age-old fables to submit to an impartial study of the natural world. This study has revealed man's gigantic, catastrophic failure to justify any special dominant place for himself.

A worldwide outcry from forgotten and oppressed millions, and from Nature herself, has forced us to face the monstrous egoism of mankind and to accept our sacred duty to redress the havoc we have created and beg to be allowed to help in the building of a new society on the ruins of the old. But we still cling desperately to the easy old and put off the difficult new. Yet this 'disease of tomorrow' can no longer be put aside or papered over. To make a new map of the times, man himself has to change, to see himself.

Has Western civilization, with its dominant belief in the outer world, had its day? Multiplying cleverness at our own mechanical, computer-god level seems to be leading us straight to self-destruction.

At the same time there is a tremendous hidden urge rising in the hearts of the silent majority, a desperate cry for leaders who see things as they are. Only such people can bring us back to the old way of honour and honesty and the place that once was offered us.

We stand on the edge of the precipice. If we jump, the only safety rope to help us is humility and prayer, trusting God's mercy and forgiveness – and our change of heart.

1

The Dilemma

'The perfection of a being depends on the quantity and quality of his inner experiencings.'

The worldwide free-for-all we see around us today holds two absolutely different kinds of people: one lot outward-looking, convinced that all problems can be solved by changing the world, the other inward-looking, certain that nothing can be solved except by changing ourselves. Of course there have always been such differences; what is unique today is that we see their vital importance, not only as world problems, but as *our* problems. The dilemma they pose is both global and personal. It is constantly before us. We cannot escape it.

The faith of the outward-lookers is founded on a firm belief that all progress depends on harnessing the world to the service of man. Their philosophy of 'more' is one of aggressive greed. Men are to be judged by what they have, not what they are. The earth is to be systematically plundered of its oil, its coal, its forests, its ocean life, of anything which can be turned to profit, all under the banner of raising the standard of living – whatever it may do to the standard of life.

Of course this philosophy of 'more' has some small gains to show. The obsession of science to get to the bottom of things has led to spectacular advances in many fields. It would be quite wrong to ignore the inquisitive zeal of research. But very often the aims seem to be questionable,

1

and while we admire the brilliance of the inventors and are grateful for the convenience and comfort they bring, we cannot escape an uncomfortable feeling that all is not well. This 'great leap forward' has not brought with it the peace, freedom from care, contentment and happiness it promised.

It is such doubts that breed the dismay and feed the questions of the inward-lookers. Are we on the wrong road? Does the fault lie 'not in our stars, but in ourselves that we are underlings'? Suppose we were to reverse the whole process, examine our feelings, our greeds, our monumental egoism. Would that help?

It is already quite evident that, as a method of creating a state of peace and prosperity, violence and force, and greed and grab simply do not work. Our materialistic money-grubbing has led us swiftly to a bankrupt world, bogged down in poverty and debt, crippled by fanatical wars and feuds, impotent in the face of murder, brutality and corruption, and at the mercy of every form of self-indulgence, laziness and waste: Sodom and Gomorrah on a global scale.

While wallowing in the general road to ruin something new, and far more serious, is slowly beginning to dawn on us. This is the doomsday thread back of it all, namely that the firing of even half a dozen nuclear weapons will secure the destruction not only of the 'enemy' but of other populations all over the world, irrespective of nationality, creed or colour, to be followed inevitably by the loss of all their live-stock and crops — to say nothing of children, born and unborn. This, the ultimate weapon of self-destruction that science has given to the world, has been made a thousand times more dangerous by the possibility of it falling into the hands of irresponsible maniacs, ignorant and careless of its effects.

So should we continue to have any confidence in politicians and dictators who still play the power game and advocate the deployment of such missiles? Do we want the entire destruction of the human race? As long as such criminality is tolerated and the futility of war accepted such suicidal horrors remain.

If Utopia seems unlikely to be reached by pursuing outward-looking material aims, at least these aims can be clearly recognized by their results, which can be labelled and quantified. Can the same be said for the inward-lookers? They seem to have some difficulty in defining exactly what they are after and, if they are clear about that, are often in dispute about the means they propose to reach it.

Everybody will agree that what we all want is a better world; but what sort of a world would that be and what sort of effort must be made to attain it? There lies the dilemma of our choice.

The dilemma is ages old. What is new is the growing willingness to begin to look at ourselves, to recognize the extent of our egoism, to accept that possibly we may be wrong. This is an enormous change; it brings an inspiring surge of hope and at the same time a sense of awe before the scale and variety of the global problems it opens up.

To see that all problems are global problems we have only to open any copy of any daily paper. Decisions taken on all manner of subjects fill the pages. All are taken in the belief that they are right and that as a result of them things will be better. But are they? After a while it usually happens that some new feature turns up which affects the steps already taken, and these almost invariably result in reversing or modifying the earlier decision.

Life is always changing. Nothing stands still and we cannot foresee the future; but the wisdom of decisions can be measured by how long they last when circumstances change. Wisdom comes from a wide and deep background of education and experience. There is not a lot of it about. Things go wrong usually because we haven't sufficiently studied the problem and foreseen the results. So one mistake leads to another and very soon chaos reigns. Finally the simplest thing, like posting a letter or making a telephone call, requires an international conference to make it work.

The fact is that, so far, when it comes to legislating on a global scale, human beings are too stupid, too selfish and too small-minded to think and work in terms of international co-operation and goodwill. A new breed of human beings must emerge, impartial and patient enough to begin to find the way to open windows and frame laws that can benefit the general good.

But this is a question of enormous difficulty. To get some idea of what is involved we have only to look at the balance and harmony achieved by Nature. In conditions of almost infinite complexity, she contrives a whole in which every creature can find a place, but subject to the most delicate and effective brakes and balances to prevent it exceeding that place. The divine will, whatever else it may be, is of such intellectual capability and capacity as to leave us awed by its majesty, its patience, its beauty and its love. If we are really longing for a better world, we have to begin to try to emulate, however ineffectually, her way of achieving harmony.

So what kind of human being is it who can begin to live his life with such aims in mind?

If a man has as his aim the idea of being useful to his fellow men he must surely start by asking himself: 'Am I the sort of man likely to be any good at it? What do I want – for myself, for my neighbour, for my fellow men?' Thinking such questions over and over, he may find himself facing a very awkward question: 'What sort of a man am I?'

There is enormous resistance to a question like that. How can I look at myself? Why should I? I'm quite all right as I am. In fact, come to think of it, what is there more fascinating than myself? And so wonderful! I know all the answers. I'm always right. I admit I do occasionally stretch it a bit. There have been situations in which maybe I did behave rather badly, and I suppose I have sometimes been a bit unjust and rude. Occasionally I admit, only to myself of course, that I'm not really quite what I pretend to be. There are things I'm not quite satisfied with. I must have a bit of a conscience some-where.

Such thoughts, turning and turning inside me, slowly face me with the truth: my everlasting contradictions and inconsistencies. Of course I do have a decent side, but scratch me and out come the claws! There! I've said it. That's how I am. That's the truth. But mind you, so is everybody else. That's how the world is.

But as I go on living with this picture, I find I don't like it. I don't like myself either – or the world that is like me: all the lying, the money-grubbing, the hypocrisy. I reject it. There must be something else, something better, some way to get out of the mess, to clean myself up. I can't be the first to think thoughts like this, but when are we all going to wake up?

2

Uncertainty

'All three-brained beings constantly carry on a relentless struggle against the wishes of their planetary bodies so that there should be formed in them from this struggle those sacred crystallizations from which their higher being parts arise and are perfected in them.'

If we say that everything runs down, that time is the universal destroyer, there is certainly nothing new about it. But what is often overlooked is that without this running down, nothing could happen. Happening is a function of time.

We can think of the future as an enormous reservoir, brimming with endless possibilities. In it anything can happen – but nothing has, as yet. As the future spills over into the present, a choice has been made. A thousand things *could* happen; but only one actually happens. It is easier to see this on a personal level. Before I came down to my study, I had the choice of going for a walk, listening to a radio programme, reading a book, helping my wife in the garden or doing some painting. I passed all these possibilities up in favour of sitting down to prepare this study for you. Out of all the possibilities, I could only choose one – a tremendous narrowing down. One thing is done at the expense of everything else. And with each choice fewer and fewer other choices are available, so finally, if this was all, everything would come to a halt. But it doesn't. Why?

We often dream of a perfect world. Perfection is a very

strong human aspiration. But perfection, as I understand it, is something complete, which we cannot, and do not wish, to alter. In that case it cannot exist in time, because it is not changing, growing, reaching out: it is there already. To be perfect is to be dead.

Our world is, and I believe is meant to be, imperfect, always in flux, offering endless possibilities of growth and decay, a constant challenge, a testing ground for the experience of living. And not only for human experience, of course. To live is to be tested in the ability to make something of a situation – what Darwin called 'the survival of the fittest'. And this process continues because another force intervenes in the universal running down of all things and that is the power life has – at least for a time – to renew itself, to wind up what has run down.

The drama, the challenge, of life lies in this renewal, in the eternal struggle to perfect something which can never be perfected. And because it is imperfect, it is always untidy, out of balance, dying down here, springing up there, full of doubts, difficulties and uncertainties. In our daily lives today we are certainly familiar with this: the unknown, the unexpected, the unwanted assault us daily. How can any of this be turned to profit?

Today we live in a very materialistic, scientific age. It has made us very arrogant and cocksure. Some are growing to believe that we have life under our belt, as to speak, and it is only a matter of time, quite a short time, before we shall discover how to create life itself. Our wonderful computers, running through all the combinations of life possibilities at lightning speed, will come up with a final solution. How can we be so naïve?

Computers have to be programmed by the fallible, limited human intelligence, so naturally the final answer does not appear. So now we are beginning to climb down a bit and wiser heads have come up with a far more humble principle to reconcile us to the idea of uncertainty, of approximation, of the universe being rather an untidy place in which everything is in movement in relation to everything else: a dance, a dream, without beginning and without end. A new vision of perfection appears. It is something caught on the wing, a momentary passing of beauty, a pause in the course of a process whose total outline must be, like our destiny, ever beyond us. We cannot predict these moments of perfection, nor can we hang on to them. They happen. If we are receptive, awake, we catch them.

All this is not too difficult applied to the natural world around us; but when it comes to our human world it is another matter, for we have something the rest of great Nature has not: reason, intelligence. A cat cannot multiply nor a horse ask questions; but human beings can and in doing so raise all sorts of problems.

Gurdjieff invites us to think of the creation as a concentric universe, a set of worlds one within the other, each in essence alike, each perfect in its own way and its own scale. Divine reason created the whole, but it also created the lesser worlds within it. Way down towards the bottom of the ladder, so to speak, stands man, a tiny world in himself with a chip of God in his heart.

It is here that the drama of our life begins because, having our own intelligences, we begin to use them. Our struggles and strivings begin to affect the divine plan itself which, since it is alive, must also grow. Our 'divine discontent' is a sort of feedback towards the source, questioning, probing, endorsing that larger order of things whose outline we dimly see, and that rarely.

We have made up so many fairy tales about our Father Creator, it seems comparatively simple to assert that His universe is growing, spreading – indeed our astronomers tell us so. So it follows that more and more beings with reason are needed to administer its complex order. Can we see here an aim in our immortality: the possibility, if we become worthy, to help in the direction of an enlarging world?

So, to recap. First, life is not, and cannot be, perfect. Perfection is something finished and life is never finished. Second, human beings collectively act as a sort of protest or comment to the Almighty which continually monitors and serves to readjust the larger plan. God has need of us as much as we have need of Him. Our longing, our discontent, our feedback is vital.

This new attitude is not easy to acquire. The old one was much more comfortable. One path led to heaven, the other led to hell. Salvation or damnation were black and white and there was little mercy for backsliders. Beliefs of this kind have existed for centuries. Nobody doubted them. They were a normal expectation.

This word 'expectation' is the key to understanding much in our attitude to life. We live on expectations. We expect to be there tomorrow. We expect to find our family around us, our usual train to be running and our colleagues there to greet us in the office. Anything that upsets these expectations is a threat to our security, our peace.

Today the old certainties no longer hold good. We may not be there tomorrow, our family may have left us, the trains may not be running and our colleagues may be on strike. An element of uncertainty has entered into everything and we begin to see that the uncertainty principle which we'd always thought of as belonging to the realms of Einstein is really basic practical everyday stuff. We live at the mercy of uncertainty.

Now this is very upsetting. It throws us. Our comfortable dream is shattered. A good deal of our effort goes into a pigheaded determination to make things conform to our expectations. We fiddle the facts to fit the dream. A great deal of our discontent, our material greed, our lawlessness today stems from this uncertainty. We don't know how to *be* before life. The comfortable chair has been pulled from under us and we are floundering. We don't know where we are. And to compensate we gorge ourselves with material things, imagining they will bring us security, certainty, peace.

But how would it be for a change, if we didn't expect anything, if we took everything fresh and new as it came to us? As if the present moment was everything — as indeed it is.

Simple to say, next to impossible to do. We have to long for that attitude so deeply it takes precedence over everything else.

But if we can't do that, we can at least ponder it, wish for it, point towards it. For the more we live in the moment, enjoy it, revel in it, the less we shall be subject to uncertainty. It is a strange paradox. If we live for now, there is no 'forever'.

3

What Touches Me?

'Great Nature has given us the possibility of being not merely a blind tool, but of working at the same time for ourselves, for our own egoistic individuality.'

Sometime or other, probably when you were quite young, you heard something or read something. And inside you there was an answer to it, a sort of call between you and the word that reached you.

But you lost it. It went. And, without quite knowing how or why, it left a vague feeling of something being missing, a lack, maybe even a hunger, for the renewal of that emotion that first touched you so long ago.

Probably with time you rationalized it. You told yourself you were far from perfect, but you did your best to listen to or read about ideas, explanations, exhortations about serious things. Good. It keeps that part of you alive – just. It's a starvation diet, of course, and your only hope is to give up starving that secret, sacred part of you and begin to feed it wholesomely and fully, as you feed your body.

Many people, when they begin to think about 'serious' things tend to get drawn into euphoric generalities, imaginary ideas and hopes which, however desirable they may be, are in fact far beyond any practical possibilities – unless? – unless we hit on the idea of a stairway, of a step-by-step approach to aims which are so far beyond us. The highest goal is always there, but today's task is to make the next step. It is an essentially practical view. We must do our elementary work,

11

groundwork, to find out more about this unknown creature we call 'I' who so naïvely wants – and even expects – to 'go to heaven'.

So, to begin, let us start to explore new ideas on how we work – the nature of our psychological anatomy so to speak. Maybe this will help us to understand why we starve what is really our most precious possession.

We all live in watertight compartments. We joke about it and say 'our right hand doesn't know what our left hand's doing' but we don't really face it as a truth, a deep and very important truth, that within what we call our life there are dozens of lives, all quite separate, private. We shall see, if we are honest, that our lives are all cut into little pieces.

Do you see what I mean? Our professional life is quite different from our domestic life. We have ties, loyalties, obligations to both. Often they are in conflict. But this is only the beginning. Look at the difference between the way we talk to the greengrocer (whom we don't like) and the way we chat with the butcher who is a friend of ours. Listen to your voice when you speak to your superiors and the one you use when you talk to those you consider inferior.

All right, you say, but what's so new in that? Everybody has different sides to themselves, different moods. When I feel differently, I behave differently. Everybody does. That's life.

Look more closely. When one of these parts is uppermost in you, where are all the others? A moment ago you were furious with your wife. An hour before you were kissing her. Now you are all anger, then you were all love.

It is this we don't see. A world of total strangers lives within us. Among the crush, one quiet unobtrusive one, squashed by all the others who live our lives for us, is the one that seeks God. Small wonder we don't hear him, can't find him.

But how is this possible? How can such a crowd live inside me and never see each other, never admit each other's existence?

We face a difficult idea – inside the self lives a whole society, all strangers to each other, hardly suspecting each other's existence, yet each labelled with my name, each calling itself 'I'. It's such a totally different way of looking at ourselves that, at first, we cannot really accept it at all.

We say 'I' have moods. That is how we excuse our contradictions – when we see them. But, if we look more carefully, we shall see each mood is total while it lasts.

Peter loved Jesus. But he denied him. When Jesus told him that he would, Peter protested it was impossible. The 'I' that loved and the 'I' that denied were total strangers to each other. Yet this Peter, this – some would say – untrustworthy man, became the rock on which the church of Christ was built. We have to accept that however teaching is brought into the world, it has to be transmitted and upheld by ordinary men, with all their frailties and contradictions.

So where is 'I'? What is it? It is impossible to catch it. It moves like lightning. At one moment it is furious, the next it is laughing. It is depressed, jubilant, envious, boastful, deceitful by turns and because each change is stamped with a sort of hallmark or label, 'I', everything is quite all right. Such is my egoism that if 'I' have said it, done it, felt it, 'I' can't be wrong.

Rationally, of course, this is absurd. If we stand back, even a little, from ourselves, we can recognize these opposites, we can admit the changes in our point of view – afterwards. But while it is all going on, what prevents us, blinds us, insulates us from our contradictions?

It is a neat piece of apparatus we learn to use as we grow up. Gurdjieff called it 'buffers'. Buffers are shock absorbers fitted to railway trucks to minimize the violence of collisions. Our buffers insulate one 'I' from another, so that without remorse or inconvenience of any kind, we contradict ourselves, deceive ourselves and lie to our heart's content, never feeling the shock or shame of it all. Alas, without one centre, one permanent 'I' to whom all can refer, it must be so. But can such a focus exist? Is it within human power to have only one 'I'? Can we be free from what the Hindus call the 'opposites'? Or is it all just Utopia, pie in the sky?

We have to face our situation. I am a world. You are a world. By moments our worlds touch. Very lightly. Very tentatively. As if we were all dressed in diving suits, heavy weighted feet, big awkward helmets, unable to do more than nod or point at one another. That's how we are – alone. Just touching the other worlds nearest to us, fingering them as they go by: friends, lovers, colleagues, enemies. . .

We know nothing about each other's worlds. The part of me that touches you at this moment is only a very small part. The part of you that reads is only a fraction of all you are. I don't tell you how I flew aeroplanes or keep bees. You don't tell me how you are writing a book or studying computers. All the rest of our worlds are hidden from each other. We are like balloons floating that lightly touch, kiss as we pass, and are gone.

Digging in your garden, have you ever turned up an ant's nest? Suddenly there before you is another world, hurrying, scurrying, totally preoccupied with its own life. Suppose that in that world there is just one ant that you want to find, only one who might listen to you. How do you find him, recognize him? It's almost impossible. It is a chance in a million that the 'I' in me that speaks to you now can meet the 'I' in you that can really listen, really wants to hear.

It wasn't always so. There was a time when the part that cared about our inner life was an important part, an accepted figure who had a big say in ordering our lives. Difficult to find him today. He's starved, forgotten, pushed aside, squashed by the noisy crowd that is rushing nowhere.

But we *must* find him. Must feed him. Must care for him, give him place, give him sun. Our lives depend on it. Not just our spiritual lives, our very physical lives and those of society depend on finding this buried part of us and beginning to listen to it, follow its lead. The alternative is disaster or death.

But suppose you've begun to see that your life is cut into little bits, that you live at odds with yourself, always fighting and arguing, what can you do about it? It doesn't do much good just to see things.

No, not true. It does more good than anything else. It is the first good.

See your contradictions. Accept that you love what you hate and hate what you love. It is bitter, humiliating; but it's the only way. Remember that lovely prayer, 'Turn thy face from my sins and wipe out all my misdeeds and create in me a new heart, O God'? A pious hope! Better to pray: 'Turn thy face towards my sins, face me with my misdeeds and the struggle and suffering that brings will itself create a new focus, a new life in me.' This is the way God works.

On the day when you have accepted all your contradictions, when all your 'I's are safely collected under the shadow of one 'permanent I', then you will have made it. The Society of Strangers has become the Society of Friends.

But you must be warned, the journey is long.

4

Something Else

'Every action of man is good in the objective sense if it is done in accordance with his Conscience and every action is bad if from it he later experiences remorse.'

This 'something else' is hidden. It does not often appear in daily life. It is strictly personal, kept behind locked doors marked 'private'. And, though we don't know exactly what it is and can't define it, in a special way it's precious. Sometimes we seem almost ashamed of it, as if it were a weakness; sometimes we are fiercely defensive about it. It is ours and nobody is going to touch it.

But however we look at it, there is certainly 'something', separate from daily living, which, whether we ignore it or not, remains like a sort of 'presence' inside us, agreeing or disagreeing with what we do or say – approving or disapproving – or just detached from our ordinary life. But if we happen to pause to refer our behaviour to this 'something else', it can set up battles so powerful and intense inside us that we quickly close the door on it. We don't like criticism, even from ourselves, and are always quick to justify everything we do.

All 'communicators' who talk about these things are very anxious to touch this nerve ending, this raw spot, and to persuade all those who can listen, *not* to shut it away, *not* to refuse to let it participate, but to accept that it is just as much part of us as the colour of our hair or the size of our feet and allow it to emerge from the secret depths of what is sometimes called the subconscious to share in, and even direct, our daily lives.

This 'something else' is called by some the heart, by others the spirit or the soul; but whatever label we put on it, it is clearly not the same part of us that buys toothpaste or drives the car. But then what is it? What is it there for? Does it really exist or is it just fantasy, imagination? And, if it does exist, and is a part of us, what use is it? Why was it put into us, so to speak?

Such questions are not necessarily religious or psychological, they are more scientific, anatomical, a matter for research. How are we made? How are we put together? Fascinating questions!

This 'something else' we all carry about with us whether we like it or not, has it a function, a use? And, if so, what is it? Should we encourage it or suppress it? And what will be the effect on us whichever we do?

It depends on the sort of life we lead. If we are entirely preoccupied with day-to-day affairs, if our lives are filled with routines of work or play and this satisfies us, then we are, in fact, living automatically, like an animal – though, of course, we should hotly deny that! In such cases we don't actively suppress this 'something else', but we effectively do the same thing by burying it so deep that it never appears. Or, to put it another way, we wear a suit of armour which completely imprisons this living part of us. Sometimes this imprisonment is actually lethal and the prisoner dies, while the so-called life continues, like an automaton, a zombie. But fortunately such death-in-life is rare. Suppression then ignores and shuts off any examination or question about this inner core we are all born with and, since we can only grow through questioning and struggling towards more understanding, this path leads nowhere.

On the other hand to encourage this 'something else', which we hardly know anything about, to participate in our daily lives, at once begins to set up frictions and questions. It begins to suggest as a right course of thought or action something very different from the way we are accustomed to think or act, and the way others about us think and act. We begin to find that our way of life is in question, and that makes everything very awkward. But, if we persist, this occasional visitor to our inner board meetings becomes an ally, a mentor, a friend.

This guide, this 'something else', which we may begin to allow to enter our lives is, in fact, our conscience. It has been called the representative of the Creator in us. It is the still small voice that occasionally nudges us to reconsider our attitudes, to revalue our values. We have to be very attentive to hear it because it is so quickly shouted down by all the ready-made judgements by which we are accustomed to live. And even when we have heard it, we cannot easily follow it because of the tremendous momentum of automatic living which absolutely repudiates any change.

Why then should anyone persist in struggling to try to hear the whispers among the shouting? I think it is because this 'something else' has validity, authority. To listen to the whispers is, we feel, somehow to have won a victory, to have chosen the better path. It is clean. We never feel ashamed of it or regret it – which is more than we can say for so many life decisions.

But isn't this saying, in effect, that there are two moralities – a human morality and a divine morality? Yes, it is.

There are two moralities, two codes of behaviour, operating in all of us. There is the code based on divine conscience hidden deep within us, difficult to find, which often seems to prompt an attitude too idealistic, too high for everyday life; and there is the common code of morality we have cooked up for ourselves, governed by man-made laws and regulations. This code (which we *call* conscience) is always changing. We cannot rely on it. To buy and sell human beings in slave markets was once a perfectly normal daily occurrence. To exile a man to Australia as a convict for stealing a sheep was considered perfectly proper. For a man to have four wives is permissible in Islam; in England it would put him in prison.

To deviate from the 'party line' means starvation, torture and exile in some countries, in others the deviation would be welcome. All these laws and regulations have been dreamed up by society or the Church or dictators, to suit their own particular motives or ends. Change the government, change the morality, change the laws. Such moralities are as fickle as fashions; they have no roots.

The morality that reaches us through the medium of this 'something else', our buried conscience, is changeless. It is enshrined, verbalized, for Jewry in the Ten Commandments: thou shalt not kill, steal, lie, envy and so on. And these negative precepts of Moses as to what a man may *not* do are balanced by the positive attitude of Jesus typified in 'Thou shalt love thy neighbour as thyself.'

In the West we all know these commandments. We were brought up with them. The difficulty is to treat these great generalities personally, to free this almost unknown, imprisoned part of us, so that it begins to vibrate to these everlasting wavelengths. How to find the honourable attitude and live it? That is the problem. It is the basis of all our problems.

It is not much help to lecture ourselves, to say we 'ought' to do this or that we 'should' not give way to the other. 'Ought' and 'should' are dream words. They do not belong to reality. To find a becoming attitude, a right action, we have to begin digging in another direction — deeper.

What we are looking for, whether we know it or not, is quietness. Quietness is the sure foundation of all hope. It is not easy to reach. It has to be fought for again and again; but, if we persist, there is no end to what we can understand from this effort. Learn to treasure your inner quietness. Make it your daily business to try, however often you fail, to reach it and bring the taste of it back into your worldly affairs. For this living presence wants to be found, longs to be found and be seen as a witness to the world that there is a source that can uphold our lives, a conscience, a godhead, from which all flows, and its messenger is this 'something else' born within us.

5

Genesis

'Every breathing creature is equally near and dear to our Common Father Creator.'

One of the theories about the creation of the universe is that space is full of cosmic dust, the prime source material out of which everything is made. It is a sort of saturated solution in which at certain points and at certain times, in response to laws we have no idea of, concentrations begin to appear and worlds are formed. From this process the whole starry heaven, galaxies and suns, crystallizes out. But at the same time erosion is always going on. Slowly the created worlds are reduced to dust again and all the time they are being recreated out of this dust. This is the ultimate struggle between life and death. Without the regenerative forces the universe would finally be reduced to chaos and darkness. The creative force we call God, to overcome the erosion of time, invented the positive force we call life and made it, like time, everlasting.

Time is itself a strange phenomenon, a mysterious simplicity. It flows always. It is irreversible. But the speed of its passing varies according to the place you see it from. We have grown accustomed to thinking of time as something 'real', which we measure by our clocks and watches; but all we are doing really is to divide one rotation of our earth into hours and minutes and its orbit round the sun into our calendar year. If, for some reason, either our orbit or the speed of our rotation were to change, our present measurements would be useless. We all know how time drags tediously when we have nothing to do and goes by in a flash when we are busy. All we can do is register the speed of passing events. They vary.

For instance, our solar system, taken as a whole, has its own specific path in space. We do not know what it is; but if it wants to measure time, it can only do so in relation to other solar systems in the galaxy. Such a time scale must be infinitely longer than ours. Time varies with the observer.

Or take the opposite extreme, the living cells in my body. If they are concerned with time, then day and night or the changing seasons are clearly meaningless to them. Their life is so short that the body in which they live seems immortal. But if they look for fixed points, they could find them perhaps in my breathing or the beating of my heart. They would measure, as we do, the rate of passing events, relating them to something which, it seems to them, will never change.

But time, the destroyer, is only one aspect. Life, the re-creator, is the other.

Life, the re-creator! Can we find, beneath its infinite complexity, basic powers, like springs, which, as it were, wind it all up and make it go?

I believe there are three main springs, a primordial, fundamental trinity that participates in the re-creation of life and makes it what it is. This trinity is compounded of reason, order and love. The three constantly interact, support and maintain each other. They are one. Yet each aspect is clearly different and can be examined separately and related to the others. Reason, order and love. Let us take reason first.

By reason I mean intelligence, the power of the divine mind to imagine and remember, to plan and execute, to co-ordinate and understand, at all levels, in a million ways, so that life *works*. And by working I understand the creation of organisms that maintain themselves and defy the running down of time, the universal destroyer.

Consider the natural world around us, the infinitely complex ecology of Nature. Everything meshes with everything else, depends on everything else, sustains everything else.

Only a reason of inconceivable ability could foresee the myriad reactions and meld them into a harmonious whole. It is a demonstration of re-creative genius, a complete understanding of the needs of everything that exists, all discharged with a majestic impartiality. A dynamic plan. The fruit of reason. Checkmate to destruction. Life conquers, endures, works.

And the wonder of the divine reason does not stop there. Take any part of Nature – a tree, a tiger or an ant – each is, in itself, a marvellous self-supporting, self-regenerating unit. It grows, it feeds, it breathes, it reproduces itself. Not only for itself, but as a part of the whole within which it exists. At every point, wherever you touch it, life is glowing with the divine intelligence, with divine reason, so all-seeing, so profound, it makes the deepest human thought a triviality.

For example, would you care to design a pump to run twenty-four hours a day for eighty years without attention? It must adjust to load and temperature, compensate for its own wear, be self-lubricating and self-cleaning, and no breaks for servicing will be permitted. By any human standards that is an impossible project. Yet we all have one and never give it a thought for the miracle it is – until it begins to go wrong!

It is one of the million fruits of a divine reason. But now, what of order?

In this trinity of reason, order and love, reason is the active, creative force, the prime motivation by which everything comes into existence. The universe had to be created to combat the destruction of time, otherwise God himself would finally cease to exist.

At our level reason can be thought of as intelligence. In the same way, we may see order as pattern, as habit. Every living thing is part of an order and has in itself a specific pattern of habits. Or, to put it another way, all life has cycles, rhythms. The sun has its spots and its flares, which follow some pattern we hardly understand; the solar system – the sun and its associated planets, asteroids and comets – has a definite pattern which we have worked out. Here in our life on earth there are clearly marked rhythms of the seasons with which we are all familiar. Lower still, man is a creature of habit. The body has its own rhythms of sleeping and waking, of eating and working. If we look closer, we can see a repertoire of gestures, habits of speech, patterns of thought which are all quite personal. Habits play an enormous part in our lives and we have little idea how powerful they are until we contradict them. Try writing or brushing your teeth with the wrong hand and you will quickly see the compulsive power of habit.

When it comes to Nature's ways, the habits and patterns of life around us, we are constantly awakened into a state of astonished bewilderment at the diversity of the creation. Everything feeds on everything else, yet everything is given its own protection, its own chance against the hunter that is born to kill it. The deer can outrun the lion, the moth is invisible on the bark, the fly can see the web. Each creature has its own pattern of defences and lives to escape death until it has given birth to the life to come.

And each pattern is individual. Every creature is what it is and does what it must do. Its order, its pattern, is fixed. Divine reason created it in the first place, made the prototype. Now order fixes it, ensures the repeat orders, the mass production.

There are mistakes, variables, uncertainties, of course. Without them there could be no change. But we do not live in a wholly whimsical, random, unpredictable universe, our world is governed by laws that are just, impartial and divine.

And what about the last member of the triad – love. It seems, at first, oddly assorted with the other two. Reason, order and love. How does love come into this basic blueprint of the construction of the universe? There is a certain affinity between reason and order. We can feel the relationship. Intelligence can show itself in order: order is an aspect of intelligence. But love . . .? It's a conundrum.

In Genesis, when God had created the world, He saw that it was 'good'. He was pleased with it, it satisfied Him. It worked. He loved His creation, as every creator should. But, because of its human associations, love is a difficult word for us. We cannot separate it from personal love, affection, sex and the rest. But 'Not a sparrow falleth to the ground without my Father' is another sort of love, nearer to the meaning given in Ecclesiastes, that is compassion, charity, something profound full of tenderness, care and pity.

Keats said 'Beauty is truth, truth beauty'. Better would be 'Beauty is love, love beauty', not connecting beauty and love in any romantic sense but as two aspects of a power that emanates from the divine.

We spoke of rhythms and patterns, of the order in life. There is always the push and the pull, the out and the in. What proceeds from the centre must return to it again, just as the rain falls and is again drawn up into the clouds. To go up, you must first go down. So this divine love issuing from the prime source must return to it again. Descending, it suffuses and saturates every particle of the creation. But the created world is also alive. It has a particle of the divine within it. It also loves after its fashion and its fashion is to manifest this love through beauty. What we call beauty is the instinctive homage of love being continuously offered up to the Creator. The roar of the lion, the fragrance of the rose, the song of the lark are the offerings of incomplete and transient beings made to the perfection out of which they sprang.

Reason, order and love act in concert together and love is a sort of divine lubricant which, entering into everything, reconciles the highest to the lowest, the many to the one, and these three forces permeate the manifested universe. It is out of this understanding that Job's chronicler celebrated the moment 'when the morning stars sang together and all the Sons of God shouted with joy.'

6

Sleep

'Remember yourself always everywhere.'

At a very early stage the student of Gurdjieff's work meets one of its most difficult ideas. It is not a new idea – every serious religion contains it. But Gurdjieff puts it forward in such a way that it becomes central to study. At the same time it demands an absolute reversal of all our previous habitual ways of thought and has to be faced and verified in our personal work. Gurdjieff puts the idea quite bluntly. He says:

> At this moment you are asleep.
> An hour ago you were asleep in bed. Your present state is practically the same. Everything you do, you do in sleep. You act in sleep, live in sleep and die in sleep. You, me, all of us from Emperor to tramp, black or white, clever or stupid, all, without exception, sleep. This is the lowest common denominator of life on earth, the chief feature of mankind.

Now of course this is totally unacceptable. We are so completely conditioned to the belief that we are not only wide awake, but even very competent and intelligent in all we do while we are awake, that any suggestion that we are not in control of our powers is instantly dismissed as nonsense, the raving of an idiot.

However, for those who can keep their cool, the proposition must be taken, not as a metaphor or allegory but as a literal statement of fact. It has been taught, I repeat, by every serious religious teacher that history records. Sometimes other words are used to convey the same idea. Those who begin to understand are urged to arise, to be alert, to be aware, to watch. The Buddha – whose very name means the awakened one – gives detailed instructions for awakening and, in the dialogues of Plato, in the Sufi tales, in Old Testament stories and, above all, in the Gospels, there are parables, incidents, all of which refer to sleep. The reproach in the Garden of Gethsemane and almost the last words of Jesus on the Cross are a prayer for forgiveness for those who *do not know what they are doing.*

So, if it is mad once again to bring this basic fact to the notice of people, it is to be mad in very good company. The wisdom of the ages is behind it.

Yet we cannot see, cannot accept it.

But consider. What happens in dreams? At the time it all seems absolutely real, yet afterwards it's absurd. Quite impossible, totally unexpected things happen. Before you get home tonight, something just as unexpected, just as unlooked for may happen to you in your 'real' life. If you woke up, you would see it.

To take the proposition that we live our lives in a state of sleep, of dreams, any further, I have to assume there are some who, though they may not have faced such an idea before, don't dismiss it out of hand. But they may very well want a more detailed explanation. So let us try to take it to pieces.

To see that I am asleep, somebody else inside me must be there to notice it. I must be divided. There is one part going about its daily business and another part observing that business. Some people find such an idea strange. They are quite unself-critical. Others are quite used to watching their own behaviour. Both kinds can recall moments in life when, under the stress of excitement or emotion, they saw themselves and their situation with extraordinary clarity. They remember every detail so clearly that they will never forget it. They were really aware of what was going on. They were awake.

But, alas, such moments are rare and, if we are honest, we

cannot fail to see the difference between this state and the way we normally go about our lives. Nobody is there. Life lives itself in us. It walks, it talks, it does business, argues, makes love – automatically. We sleep. And because there is nobody to watch what goes on, the most terrible things go on. We can see them around us today.

But once we have seen this, really seen it, there is a hope that we may not slip back into entire forgetfulness as we were before. We begin to long to be awake, always awake. But this is terribly difficult. It seems easy, but it constantly eludes us. We forget. We can't see our sleep while we are asleep. So we give up – and the world is as it is.

This is the reason for the austerities that surround the religious life. Submission and discipline are necessary for men to attain what they seek. The Kingdom of Heaven is a pearl of great price; you cannot have it for nothing.

At this point you may say: 'I take your point. I respect such serious intention. For those who can follow it, it is valid. But I am not one of them. I don't feel called to it – and yet I am dissatisfied with my life, the way I live. Is there nothing I can do?'

Those who are still seriously trying to grapple with the idea that we live in a world of illusion, of sleep, will surely have seen that it is the deepest of all human problems. Yet, if the greatest teachers the world has known have failed to wake us up, where can we turn for help? This is what Gurdjieff has called 'the terror of the situation'.

It was not always the situation. Life goes in cycles. There was, we are told, a golden age, a time when all men and women recognized their predicament and struggled with it, a time when life flowed in a single river, when the inner and outer life were truly and harmoniously balanced. But that was before life on earth took a wrong turning. Thereafter it began to flow in two streams: those who struggled to *be*, and those who couldn't be bothered. The one stream flows into the ocean, the other is lost in the underworld. Gradually this dichotomy worsened and today everything we think important lies in the exterior world, and the invisible world, which governs the *kind* of life we lead, is ignored.

But someone will rightly ask: 'Why should waking up make any difference? Why should just *seeing* my behaviour alter that behaviour?'

It is because waking is a sacred act. Mysteriously, another level of life and conscience, which has all the time been dormant within us, starts to stir. When conscience begins to participate in our actions and judgements, they cannot remain the same. It is not so easy to lie and covet, to steal and kill, when there is someone watching what we do. Our shame begins to revolt us. We begin to see ourselves for what we are.

So this struggle to awake is a difficult and dedicated task. Those who undertake it do so in the name of all men. Those who fail in following have the lesser duty, to encourage and strengthen and respect those they cannot emulate, for they are the bearers of the world's deepest hope.

Remember that endearing, honest backslider in the Gospels who cried to Jesus 'Lord, I believe: help thou mine unbelief!' He speaks for all who struggle.

7

The Hackney Carriage

'Everything without exception does itself in contemporary man and there is nothing whatever contemporary man himself does.'

Some people tell us we oughtn't to think about ourselves. They say it's unhealthy, morbid, introspective and no good can come of it. Others say it's better not to think at all. Thought, they say, is man's greatest enemy and responsible for all our ills. Drop the mind, if you want to be happy! We are all searching in one way or another to find recipes for happiness or security; but it seems to me we can't get very far with any of them until we have begun to understand *what* wants to be happy or secure. To do that we must understand our own human mechanism. 'Know thyself' remains the first and greatest commandment.

To help men towards self-knowledge, Gurdjieff at one point proposes a very striking analogy or parable to help to clarify the way we are put together. He suggests we are all no more than horse-drawn carriages, hackney carriages as they used to be called, consisting of a cart, a horse and a driver, together with a passenger or fare, sitting in the carriage. This passenger we usually call 'I'. The carriage corresponds to our body, our emotions or feelings are the horse and the driver, sitting on the box, is our head. Let me repeat that. The driver is our head, the horse our feelings, the carriage the body and the fare who has hired it is what we call 'I'. The fare, of course, can jump in, drive off in any direction he pleases and get off where he likes.

The more you think over this strange picture of man, the more you will find in it. The idea that every human being consists of separate parts, each quite different, each with its own function, is striking. But it's true. My body lives one way and my emotions and my head both function quite differently. Yet all these three parts have somehow got to get along, to work together. This is the way we are. And then there's this idea that I'm a sort of taxi – it's preposterous at first! One fare climbs aboard and orders me to the office, then somebody else takes his place and I'm off to see the girlfriend, then there's a man who remembers he's got to buy a shirt and another who rushes me off to make a long distance call to his mother. So it goes, all day long. A hundred different impulses appear, take charge and, for the moment, command the whole of me. Then they step off the cab and somebody else turns up.

If you try to apply this analogy to yourself during the coming day you will see it all happening. How your body, the carriage, is carried about here and there, how your head always depends on your feelings, and so on.

When you first meet the idea that your body is just a cart or carriage, something that is dragged out, it doesn't seem to fit at all. Most of us think our bodies are all-important; our feelings, our heads are just part of the body, the body is the source of everything. But if you can begin to think of your body as just a complex mechanism – which it is – then it may start to look different. Suppose I want to run a record mile or climb a mountain or fight an enemy, then it's *I* want to run, *I* want to climb, I want to fight. My body just follows, obeys, carries out my orders – sometimes reluctantly. Old people know very well how the body has to be driven even to carry a bag or climb a flight of stairs. The body is always passive. It is carried by the feelings, directed by the thoughts. It is the patient servant of our every whim or folly, however much we maltreat it.

This carriage of ours is, after all, quite a complex mechanism. It has shafts and springs, wheels and bearings. Different sorts of materials go into its construction. It was designed originally to travel over rough roads. It goes better when it is used, exercised. But today when it always runs on asphalt roads, it never gets shaken up and, as the system of its greasing depends on this, it soon begins to stiffen up. Then it starts to rust, parts have to be taken apart and replaced and this is often costly or even impossible.

We can all recognize this as quite a fair picture of how our bodies behave, how lazy they are, how obstinate and how they are constantly in and out of the repair shop. A complex and costly organization exists to keep our carriages on the road and quite a number of skilled mechanics in the business have said that if only people would take practical steps to service and maintain their carts properly, half the repairs and overhauls could be avoided.

Mind you, a lot of effort goes into tarting up the outside, spraying, varnishing and titivating that part of the show – in fact a huge industry exists to do nothing else; but that doesn't help much. It's the mechanism that matters.

Now all the care of the carriage – keeping it clean, greased and in good repair – should be the business, the duty, of the driver. After all, it's his carriage. He is responsible for it. Our driver, the head, is the part of us intended to guide and care for our body, to keep the carriage roadworthy; but he doesn't seem to see it, doesn't get around to it. Why?

In this parable of the cart, horse and driver, the driver – the head – holds a unique position. He alone can speak! He alone can communicate with other drivers, find his way about, exchange news on how the world wags – in short, he alone has what we can call intelligence. Now that he drives a vehicle plying for hire, it is he who has to put up with the fares, humour them and often help them when they get lost and don't know where to go. But he's simple and uneducated, he's never really bothered to try to better himself. This is how Gurdjieff describes him:

Like all coachmen in general he is a type called 'cabby'. He considers himself competent even in questions of religion, politics and sociology; with his equals he likes to argue; those who he regards as his inferiors he likes to teach; his superiors he flatters, with them he is servile; before them, as is said, he stands 'Cap in hand'.

The desire for tips has gradually taught him to be aware of certain weaknesses in the people with whom he is dealing and to profit by them; he has automatically learned to be cunning, to flatter, to stroke people the right way and, in general, to lie.

On every convenient occasion and at every free moment he slips into a saloon or bar where over a glass of beer he daydreams for hours at a time or talks with a type like himself or just reads the paper.

This picture, however ludicrous, of contemporary man has arisen because the three parts of him, though each quite different, have never been educated to work together, live together and mutually assist and strengthen each other. On the contrary, each lives its own life, which often seems aimless, and when a concerted effort of heart, head and body is required it usually fails to appear – no training or education having been prepared for it.

This picture of man may appear a gross caricature to many. This is because even the most modest among us are so preoccupied with our own ideas, our own points of view, that we have almost entirely lost the ability to, as it were, stand back and look at our own behaviour. We get in our own way. We block our own view of ourselves. But if it should be possible for you – and I pray for your sake that it may – to begin to stand aside, to look at yourself as though you were another person, as God might look at you, then, beginning to see and accept yourself as you are, you will stand, believe me, on the threshold of a new life.

But now – the most difficult is yet to come! We have taken a look at our bodies and heads, the cart and the driver, but what about the horse? After all, what's the good of a carriage and a driver without a horse to draw them? But the horse, our feelings, there's a conundrum for you!

The first thing that is clear about the horse is that if he is obstinate or bloody-minded or just plain lazy, carriage, coachman and passenger are absolutely stuck. Unless the horse will pull, nothing can happen. The coachman may know exactly how to get to his destination. The brain may see everything quite clearly. But if the feelings aren't engaged, the thing gets nowhere. What happens in all the high-powered conferences and summits? Splendid agendas are worked out; but if everybody doesn't feel the same about the subjects under discussion, nothing goes through.

On the other hand, if the horse bolts, as in madness or hysteria, the whole outfit can be wrecked. Either way it is clear our feelings are the most important and powerful part of us. Strangely we don't seem to see it. We hear of lots of attempts to educate the head, but whoever heard of educating the feelings?

Certainly not our cabby, he doesn't give a damn about the horse. He never gives it any more than water and straw, so the poor creature is lonely, half starved and miserable. He can't pull the carriage at more than walking pace, even when he's beaten. But when you see the feelings playing like a fountain, when you hear poets singing or watch lovers dancing, you may be sure somebody has been feeding the horse and when you do that he is ready to gallop to the ends of the earth for you.

Today our bombastic cabby has a swollen head, wears a top hat and a chrysanthemum in his buttonhole and thinks there's nobody on earth like him. The whole world is in love with its supercharged head. But it's getting the world into a chaotic mess. Good healthy feelings are starved, derided; but it seems nobody cares and anything goes. In the end it all comes back to feeding our horse, that is honouring and educating our feelings.

And how do we do that? There's only one way. To return vigorously and whole-heartedly to the old truths we have derided and thrown out, that is to respect wisdom and justice, courage and moderation, to honour the Ten Commandments and the Sermon on the Mount, to serve God and keep His commandments, which is the whole duty of man.

This is what it means to feed the horse. The cheap bad food has almost starved him. He feels almost nothing. But if we don't give him intensive care – and quickly too . . . well, have we forgotten Hiroshima?

But beyond all this, what is the purpose for which the carriage exists – to carry the passenger, who, as I said, we usually call 'I'? Because we are all taxis, the fare is always changing. Our desires and inclinations, our needs and demands, get in and out of the carriage all day long. We have no permanent passenger, no owner, who commands and directs our lives.

To have such an owner, such a master, to give up this slavish vagabond life, is the aim of all those who see their plight. For there is the possibility of a permanent 'I' who could be the director of our lives, the active principle of all our struggle, the divine manifestation of God in us, the word made flesh – in a word a conscience.

8

Eat or Be Eaten

'To *do* means to act consciously and by one's own initiative.'

Have you ever thought what a macabre mystery the act of eating is? Something has to die for something else to live. Some food, vegetables, fruits, we eat raw, that is to say we eat them alive; but most of our food is other living beings that are just dead. Most animals are the same: some kill and eat at once, others eat later, still others eat what we call 'rotten' food. But everything in one way or another lives on everything else, life at the price of death. In no more final way are we members one of another.

Our bodies are the most wonderful chemical factories, which take in dead things and transform them into life, that is, into energy. By this energy we live. What we cannot transform we eliminate and this becomes food for other classes of life. We are all transformers of energy. But we should note that in the whole earthly creation, human beings are the only creatures that can live beyond the body. All the rest of the creation exists to be what it is, to maintain and re-create itself − that is, it lives for food and sex, for *this* life. Great Nature is without dreams or questions, hopes or regrets. It glories in being what it is.

We human beings have much more complicated and sophisticated chemical factories. We have spare energy, energy left over when we have satisfied our hunger for food and sex. From this some men begin to question, to hope, to require something more from life. It is the hallmark of humanity.

Our 'ordinary' food – the only food which we, in general, call food – exists to nourish only the physical self. It provides all we need to live as animals, to propagate the species and take our place in the complex of Great Nature. But this is not enough for us. This is where the mystery of human beings grows.

It begins with a divine mystery which makes men want to change things, to smash what exists to make something better. But where does it spring from? Why are we blessed and cursed with this possibility?

I think it is because humanity is irrevocably dedicated to the future. Our divine discontent, our desire to build Jerusalem in this green and pleasant land, is something that does not belong to the animal. It originates somewhere else. It seems part of some deep longing which we somehow materialize out of the air. This is nearer the truth than it seems at first sight, for air, which is our essential food also, seems to be the natural abode of the insubstantial, the longing for freedom, for perfection. Possibilities spring from the air, not from the earth. We can live without 'stomach' food for weeks, without 'lung' food not for minutes. Then what part of us does air feed? What need does it satisfy?

We usually think of 'food' in quite a narrow sense. We need to broaden the concept. A long time ago the Bible told us that man could not live by bread alone. It is literally true. Man takes in three kinds of food, each quite different from the other. The first food goes through our stomachs, the second – which we normally don't think of as food at all – through our lungs. It is this we might think about today. It is very important food. Cut it off and we are dead in two minutes.

Now air is itself a deep mystery. It is food of quite another level to the food we eat. It does not belong to the earth, though it surrounds it. It does not grow off roots; in fact it does not grow at all. It has no form. You cannot see it. Yet it penetrates everywhere. You cannot get rid of it. A pure vacuum is impossible. In addition it has no boundaries, you cannot confine it to a shape. It is always on the move. It carries the clouds and the rain. It continually cleanses and purifies itself. It is everywhere the same. It is the symbol of freedom and yet it is a protective shield saving all life from the lethal radiations of outer space.

Air is no respecter of persons, utterly impartial. It offers the same food to everyone all over the earth. It is food we do not have to labour to acquire, it is provided free, with boundless generosity, to the whole earthly creation. It is a true symbol of the divine compassion.

Now, while I am writing this, this air is entering into every living thing. Some is absorbed, some transformed, some rejected, and the next moment the residue is exhaled. All this is continually going on, from birth to death, and we do not give it a thought. It is absolutely automatic in us. Nevertheless wonders are going on. Part of this air is essential to give added impetus to our digestive processes so that substances that remain after elimination can be further refined to nourish our brains and our reproductive organs.

But more than this, air itself can be transmuted within the body if it is absorbed in a special way. Religious teachings tell us that it is possible to create a refined body within the flesh body, sometimes called the spiritual body or the astral body or the body Kesdjan. Those who wish can, by the conscious absorption of air, find their way to the possibility of creating, in this life, an inner life. This may exist – at least for a time – after the destruction of the self we know.

But beyond this wonderful possibility coming to us by the breath of life, there is still a third food to give us further nourishment.

The tiger is not more important than the gazelle it devours. The cow is not superior to the grass it crops. All living things are equally dear to our Father Creator and have their function in the collective life of the whole. But what is the function of man?

Perhaps something may have struck you about the wonder

and mystery of food. For instance, why should the life of other living beings be shortened for *me* to live? Am I worthy of what I accept as my right? Often, in the evening when I bring my day before the scrutiny of our Impartial Observer, I have to admit I have not deserved my life today. I have not lived as a man can live.

Because life itself is our third food, the richest and most powerful of all food and, in the form of impressions, influences, experiences, we are eating it all the time. Sometimes it comes at us with terrifying ferocity, sometimes with idyllic sweetness and peace; but we cannot refuse it. We must eat. All the time it is a challenge to our digestion, offering choices, possibilities, riches. How best to live, to react, to function? Honestly, dishonestly? Bravely, cowardly? Angrily, patiently?

It is like some huge supermarket. Everything is on offer. Many don't discriminate, just take what comes to hand; but you can, to some extent, choose a healthy diet and, in a very strange way, even the poorest, bitterest food can nourish you if you know how to digest it. The function of man – and the future of man – lies in the choice of his spiritual diet. So beware of the kind of life you choose.

We live by three foods. First, the coarse material food for our bellies. Secondly, the invisible and everywhere-present air, which constantly enables us to be reconciled to our experience and to choose. Thirdly, the feast of life itself, without which we could not live for a second.

Air stands between my body and my life. It is a sort of referee, an adjudicator, with a very sensitive digestion which helps me to choose the *kind* of life I lead. It is the domain of spiritual growth.

We are offered an inexhaustible cornucopia of life, to eat, to breathe, to grow by. But there is a strange and deep enigma here. Such as we are, we cannot experience the wealth that life offers. Life, our third food, is shut out. We keep it on the threshold of our lives, so to speak, and will not let it enter. Some, the tireless, lucky ones who have learned how to let it come in, will tell you that while it was admitted, everything was made new. Such rewards are the fruit of longing and patience and love.

Respect your foods. Do not take them for granted. Remember, in the widest sense, you are – and must be – what you eat.

9

A Warning

'At your age it is indispensably necessary that every day at sunrise, while watching the reflection of its splendour, you bring about a contact between your consciousness and the various unconscious parts of your general presence.'

D o you ever get fed up at the way life pushes you around? All day long we are on the run. 'I haven't time to do that', 'I shall be late for this', 'I can't possibly fit that in', and so on and so on. And all the time something inside is in revolt, doesn't want to be run off its feet, wants to get its breath, to pause, to be quiet. Most of us seem to have too much to do and not enough time to do it in.

It is this inner revolt against our life situation which builds up our dissatisfactions, our worries, our fears. It is a battlefield of contradictions. We are at war with ourselves and from this come our tensions that bring on our headaches, our breakdowns, our so-called 'civilized' diseases. What we are really doing is wasting our energy, spending our lives faster than we can make them. Mental energy, nervous energy, takes far more out of us than a day's hard physical labour. Our lifestyle is bad, but we cannot escape it. Somehow or other we have to cope.

This state of affairs has become pretty generally recognized and there are well known methods of countering it. Sometimes it is drink, sometimes drugs, sometimes tranquillizers, all are methods of relaxing, as we call it, all are attempts to forget or escape situations which are really beyond our control. The trouble is that these so-called remedies are not remedies. They wear off and we are back with the problem and besides this, the remedy often turns out to be more lethal than the disease.

But there are, of course, other ways out of this dilemma, ways that have been known for centuries to any who follow a religious life. They are called contemplation, meditation, prayer and so on. Their object is just the same, to quiet us. They require a bit more effort; you can't buy them over the counter. But they insist, with a lot of authority and after centuries of experience, that they are viable ways out of the dilemma and that, if we follow them, we can free ourselves from our problems, our miseries, our contradictions.

More recently various movements have begun to detach these remedies from their context and to regard them as a therapy which has nothing to do with the ethic from which it comes. Relaxation and meditation, they say, have nothing to do with religion. It is simply a means of damping down our minds, our emotions, and recharging our batteries.

Many of you no doubt have heard about these methods of 'self-calming'. They are certainly less harmful than drugs or drink. The old ways, we are beginning to see, turn out not to be quite so stupid as the 'know-all' world of today thought they were. But the question is: can we take them out of their context, just make use of them? And if we do, will they last any longer than drugs or drink? If they do last, if they do begin to help us, shall we not, do we not, find that, in spite of ourselves, they begin to lead us towards different states and questions about life which we have never come up against before? We have, as it were, heard a bell without knowing where the sound came from.

Anybody who has attempted exercises in relaxation, even for quite a short time, comes up against an unexpected difficulty: he forgets to do it. He may sit down with the very best intentions and start 'meditating' in some way that has been suggested to him, but within a short time he will find that he is miles away, daydreaming about a million things which have nothing whatever to do with quieting himself. The mind is very artful and has a thousand tricks to prevent us doing what we want to do, because what we want to do is foreign to the way it works.

Now this is a real difficulty. It is not easily overcome. And, because of it, right at the very outset, we start finding out about ourselves. We are forced to see that we cannot put – and keep – our attention where we want to. We have little *voluntary* attention. Normally we only attend to things that interest us. 'Things' hold our attention. We don't attend, we are attended to, so to speak. We are attended to, enslaved by, whatever comes up. To see this is an enormous discovery and it can lead us very deep; but the point I want to make now is that to relax seriously, whatever the technique, you have to *want to do it* and maintain that want when it begins to get difficult, as it certainly will.

But let us assume that we are serious and determined to try to get help this way. Let us assume that the techniques we have been taught are helpful and do succeed in chaining the wild dogs of our thoughts and keeping them in the kennel. Then certainly we shall experience a change of state and this change of state will have certain physical effects on the body itself which can be, and have been, measured.

Recently quite a lot of research has gone into the physical effects of relaxation and it has been found – and it is pretty obvious really – that relaxing can reduce the rate of breathing, slow the heartbeat, damp down mental anxiety and even reduce blood pressure. All this is to the good and all of it is to be expected since, in a quiet state, the body is relatively inactive and this is reflected in its metabolic rates.

Now if you love your body, respect your body and care for its welfare, all this is to be desired; but it is not, in itself, enough. For hand in hand with your quietness will come questions, states in which you will need help and direction. If it is not available you may become alarmed and give up, or, and this is more likely, you may lose interest in the whole thing, find it too difficult and time-consuming and revert to a pill or a stiff whisky. And this would be a pity, for you are on the threshold of something big. So what is to be done?

Nothing I have said is meant to discourage any attempts you may make towards relaxation. On the contrary, anything of this kind is highly desirable. But we must not be naïve. There are pitfalls which it is better to avoid, and they are not immediately obvious.

In daily life everything seems equally important – or unimportant. Everything competes for our attention – and is at once forgotten. You think, for instance, that you are interested in what I am saying. In a few moments you will have completely forgotten it. For anything to be remembered there has to be a real *need* for it. And need is always tied up with *aim*. My aim, I say, is to get rid of my tensions, I *need* to, therefore I will relax.

Now the first difficulty in doing so I have mentioned already. I forget to do it. I forget to do it *even while I am doing it*! I slip away. At first, while the idea is new to me, I may manage to let go for a little; but as I get used to trying it, it becomes more and more difficult. I try to remember my wish. I tell myself: 'This will really help my daily life.' But the days go by and I don't see much in the way of results. I seem to get as much caught up in things as ever. And of course I expect everything to change for me immediately, if not sooner.

But suppose I see that this does help me, that it is beginning to work. Then something else begins to happen too. I start by seeing how tense I am, how my limbs, my emotions, my thoughts are all uptight. And from that I begin to see how I am living. Getting rid of tensions means getting rid of a whole way of life. It is as if the door had been opened to show me a marvellous view, or gulf at my feet, according to the point of view. I'd been looking for results; but these were not the sort of results I'd expected.

I had started out thinking that relaxation was a sensible idea. I'd read a book about it and it sounded like a useful therapy that I could indulge in, use, like any other therapy. And now it starts to put my whole life in question. It has turned into a crossroad, perhaps the most important crossroad in my life. But I can see trouble ahead. If I decide to carry on, where will it all lead me? I shall certainly need help.

Here a word of warning is necessary. All sorts of people are ready and willing to take care of your inner life. Some are genuine, others very impressive, persuasive and possibly bogus, preying on the simplicity of people in these matters for the sake of power or money. So when you come, openly, with your search, with your hope, come also with your head on your shoulders – your ability to smell a spiritual rat, so to speak. Test the truth of what is said to you, quietly, deeply, against your need.

Relaxation is one of the main gates to the Kingdom of Heaven; but beware of the side turnings that lead nowhere.

10

A Week of Meditation

'In order to be in reality a just and good altruist it is inevitably required first of all to be an out and out egoist.'

This series of daily meditations was broadcast on the BBC World Service in 1967.

SUNDAY

You have never heard my voice before. You don't know me. You never will know me. I don't know you. I never shall know you. Yet – here I am, in your house! Isn't it extraordinary? I am uninvited. You are my host. You have permitted me to enter. A flick of the switch and you can dismiss me. I like that. I am really only happy to be where I'm wanted. Could I stay just three minutes before moving on?

Where are you now? I don't mean outside. Inside. You are probably in your thoughts. What I say comes in at your ears and goes to your head. But suppose you had toothache, where would you be then? In your tooth. The pain in your tooth would be your focus; that is where you would be. Or suppose something wonderful had happened and you were filled with joy, where would you be then? Or there had been a tragedy in your family and you were heavy with grief, then where would you be? Grief and joy attack our solar plexus,

45

'our bowels turn to water' as the Bible has it, our knees give. Feelings are not in the head.

So really we can *be* in many different parts of ourselves: in our hearts, in our stomachs, in our sex. We, as it were, move about the body and live in different parts of it. Actually we live in every cell of it – but we don't know that. We have lost touch with ourselves. We have got into the way of always living in our heads. Everything that happens, all our impressions, feelings, sensations, experiences, all get, as it were, translated into words and transferred to the head. And, since the feelings and sensations know nothing of words, it is a very poor translation. Try! Try to describe a feeling or sensation in words and you'll soon see how inadequate it is.

MONDAY

All right! Suppose we are a mystery to ourselves, suppose the admonition 'Know thyself!' is finally impossible, we can't really leave it at that. If we agree that the Kingdom of Heaven is within us, then we must be sensible, practical and begin to dig for our own treasure. If we do, we shall soon begin to pick up things in the first few steps.

Yesterday we spoke of living in different parts of ourselves. We can see how these impressions that drive us into different parts of ourselves can be divided into three main categories – our thoughts, our feelings and our sensations. We can even begin to see some of their characteristics. Thought, for instance, enables us to compare abstract ideas and set them in order. This is better than that. That is better than something else. Thought enables us to compare, to choose and thus to have direction, to formulate plans and aims. It is this faculty that separates us from the animals, for these are powers they do not have. Feelings – fear, anger, pleasure, fatigue – when we say them over like this are evidently not susceptible to reason. Maybe our head tells us it is stupid of us to be afraid or angry or tired – but we are! Emotions have no pros or cons; they are total for as long as they last. Sensations are different again, though often confused with feelings. Pain is a sensation, though we often talk about 'feeling' it. So is heat or cold. Hearing, seeing, tasting, smelling, these are all sensations.

But, of course, everything is connected, related to everything else. My reason tells me that man is talking nonsense. It stirs up my feelings. I grow angry. I sense my fists clenching and my muscles tensing. Probably I don't realize all this; but that is the mechanism of it – and if I am serious in wishing to know myself, I must try to begin by understanding something of the mechanism – as a mechanic knows an engine.

If this were all, it would be relatively simple; but the whole thing is infinitely complicated by a sort of virus that has somehow got into it – imagination. We have imaginary pains, imaginary fears, and worse still, our heads are full of imaginary situations, fancied wrongs, vain hopes – all of them lies and all of them interfering dreadfully with the normal functioning of the machine. Why do we live in such a miserable state?

TUESDAY

Why is it that all the religious teachers, all the sages, all the wise men have insisted that ordinary folk like you and me live in this imaginary world we were talking about yesterday, in this state they call the 'world of illusion'? If there is a real world, why do we prefer a dream world and obstinately continue to live in it? And why do all the teachers desperately call on us to come out of it? This is what all religion is about and, although man invents a million reasons for evading the call, what he is called upon to hear is neither complicated nor beyond him.

He is required to see – to see, mind, not to change or give up, only to see – his own situation, his real situation. What prevents him is his egoism, his pride, his self-importance, which utterly distorts it. Why cannot he give all this up? Because he is fascinated, riveted, hypnotized, by this home-made image of himself. He is like the beggar in the *1001*

Nights whom the Caliph took and sat on his throne for a day, telling him he was King. The poor man believed it and strutted about while the court laughed at him behind their sleeves. Then the night came and he was cut down and forgotten.

How can a man begin to escape from this make-believe, this grotesque idea that he is the centre and everything re-volves round him? It starts with a thought. What do I need to escape? For if I am dissatisfied with this life, I must need something. What? It can be formulated in many ways: to find the truth; to be made whole; to escape; to be master of myself. The formulation really does not matter. If I wish to move, to escape, I must first know where I am. I must know my situation. I assume I know it, but I don't. For my journey is within myself. If I set out from an imaginary position how can I ever reach a real destination. I am like that beloved sinner in the Gospels who cried: 'Lord, I believe; help thou mine unbelief!'

WEDNESDAY

It is not perhaps quite so much a journey as something urgent. Let us change the metaphor: it is more an escape from the prison in which I find myself. Of course, some never suspect they are in prison. They are happy and content shut up. Some have altogether escaped. They are happy outside. But for those inside who have not yet escaped, it is not an easy situation. For although the open country can be seen over the walls, the prison is well guarded. Barbed wire and watch-towers and worse, the inexorable relentless pressure of fellow prisoners urging us to give up the whole foolish idea – how can we hope to escape when the forces confronting us are so great? Everything is on the side of things as they are. But no; it is not like that. What is the meaning of the story of David and Goliath if it is not that the odds do not matter, that the sling of energy and the pebble of hope can defeat the monster.

For we must understand so as not to be discouraged and

cast down: only one small part in us wishes to do battle. Only one part knows; the rest neither know nor care. And do not think that the battle once fought is over. It is continually renewed. And the alternative to victory is not defeat, nor surrender. It is far more subtle than that. It is the insinuation that things are not so bad, that I am very busy today and it will be far better if I put off the fight till tomorrow.

So, even if we have once had the wish to fight, we contrive to put it off, from tomorrow till tomorrow, until one day – a sorrowful day for us, indeed – we find that we no longer have the will or the strength to escape, the time allotted to us by Great Nature having been wasted in dreams.

THURSDAY

Tomorrow! It is perhaps our greatest hope and yet it is our greatest trap. We are always looking forward to something in which we place our hopes. Generally it is tinted with rosy spectacles. It is rather the same with what has passed. I look back and what I remember may be rose-tinted too. Alternatively, of course, I may view the future with fear and doubt and remember the past with loathing and disgust. There is only one thing common to all these feelings – they are always wrong! Have you ever gone over some incident in the past with a friend who shared it? The difference between what people remember and what took place is often extraordinary. To a third person they might be talking about two different events. What really happened? Both you and your friend can't both be right.

Similarly with the future. Verify it for yourself. How do you imagine that business appointment will turn out, that romantic date, that bridge party? How will you feel, what do you intend to say, how will you come out? Tomorrow evening check yourself. Did the thing actually turn out as you confidently expected it would?

If we are honest and dispassionate about it, we have to recognize that neither the past nor the future are as we think they were or hope they may be. In a rough and ready way we know all this — and somehow it doesn't bother us. Yet it commits us to living and dying in a dream! But such a thought we violently repudiate, so strong is our illusion of being awake. But awake in what? In a future we cannot foretell or a past we cannot recall? Or awake in *now*? Now is the only moment we can actually grasp. Now is where we stand — on the very lip of Niagara, with the future rolling up, turning at our feet and roaring away into the past. We can't see up the river for mist and down the river for spray. All we could see — if we really wish — is *now*!

FRIDAY

There is only one thing about tomorrow of which we can be sure. It will be the same as today — for us, that is. When we look at our personalities, we can recognize, perhaps, that we have a certain shape. We have likes and dislikes, ideas and habits, and all these things make us what we are. So each of us is rather like a key, which we fit into the doors of life. But we have no master key: we can only open certain doors. Others are shut to us. The stockbroker cannot get into the painter's room; the key that fits the plasterer's lock will not open the hairdresser's. And so it is with us. Far more subtle and complex, of course, the more so because we have never paused to look at ourselves in this way; but basically we all carry our own keys and know the doors. We do not change. So, whatever the outward appearance of tomorrow, we shall always react in the same way towards it, always open the same doors.

Businessmen understand this very well. From a study of the past they have a clear idea of how things will go in the future. They know the trends, the form, the seasonal adjustments and so on. From a study of the past, they know the future cannot alter — unless they do something *now*! If they want to change tomorrow, *they must change it today*.

All this seems quite normal when we apply it to business,

but strange and unacceptable if we apply it to ourselves. Yet it is every bit as true. If I hope to change tomorrow, I must change today. It will not change by itself. Everything will inevitably be the same, because I am the same.

Once I see this a sense of urgency may appear. Time is counted against me. I have only so much. If I waste it I cannot get it back. If I am serious and dissatisfied, if I desire something to bring a richer hope into my life, a deeper understanding, then I must fight this disease of tomorrow and start today.

SATURDAY

Here is the end of the week and how little has been said! I feel like Carter when he first looked through that tiny hole into Tutankhamun's tomb. He knew he had stumbled on something unique, which had been hidden there for centuries. 'What do you see?' 'Marvellous things!' Dazed and dazzled at first he began to explore carefully, delicately, all those undreamed-of wonders.

When a man makes a discovery like that, he doesn't just give it an occasional thought and go on living as before, he is consumed with curiosity, with desire, to know the extent and wealth of his find. Hitherto he has only dreamed about it, now his search has been rewarded and the reality exceeds his wildest hopes.

So it is we should begin to settle down to serious study. We dare not be carried away by the wonder, though it is there before our eyes. That is for amateurs. We are students and we start with an empty notebook and begin to fill it with quite prosaic entries, the names of objects, their descriptions and apparent use, their relationship and where they are found. We know that everything we examine is precious. Nothing is too small to escape our attention. So we carefully and patiently begin the exploration of our inner world.

Of course there are always technical advisers on hand, archaeological experts who, by previous experience, can help to identify the finds and help us to put them in order. But the discoveries are ours, the assessment ours and the results ours. It is *our* collection.

So, if I am lucky enough to find the chink in the wall of my life, it would be quite irresponsible to go back to my careless ways, to the fairy stories, the make-believe. This is real. It begins to affect my attitude to life, it alters my sense of values, it gives me a new centre of attraction. I, as it were, gravitate to a wish for understanding.

It is this wish to understand that brings change with it, almost as a byproduct. I cannot set out to change my life; but if I begin to try to understand it, it may change because of that struggle.

> Here is the time gone by, and I have not stirred! The key not turned in the lock, the Guide at my elbow ignored, the treasure before me disdained! And tomorrow there will be one day less! Quicken me, quicken me, O God!

11

The Gadarene Swine

'They do not consider that at that period . . . the transmission of ideas and thoughts was still what is called . . . allegorical.'

When I first came to the study of the teaching of Gurdjieff one of the most striking of the new ideas was what is often called 'multiplicity'. It was, for me, an absolutely new idea. It made sense of human behaviour, for the first time, in a striking way. That each of us was not one person, whole, monolithic, but a mixed bag of all sorts of contradictory, irreconcilable people, all inhabiting one body, each saying 'I' and speaking as if for the whole, was a revelation.

And then one day when for some reason or other I was studying the Gospel of St Mark, I came to the story of the Gadarene swine. Such a strange story, a sort of fairy tale. At the ordinary level it really made no sense, but could there be an allegorical meaning behind the words?

I kept on thinking about it, trying to get myself back into the way they thought in those days and then, suddenly – it was like discovering America – I saw that here, 2000 years ago, in the Gospels, was this very same idea of multiplicity which I had thought so new.

St Mark tells us that when Jesus had crossed the sea he came to the country of the Gadarenes and immediately met 'coming out of the tombs a man with an unclean spirit'. The story goes on to tell how this man was uncontrollable. People had tried to chain him up, but he always broke loose.

Nobody could tame him. Whether he was up in the mountains or down in the tombs he was always raving and 'cutting himself with stones'.

If we take all this as an allegory, we can fairly interpret it to mean that this man who lived 'in the tombs', lived among dead things, material things, of no spiritual worth. He was in himself a man with an unclean spirit, otherwise what is often called a 'miserable sinner'. Nothing could 'tame' him, get him to see that there was another way to live. He was completely egoistic, wilful, listening to nobody and going his own way. Night and day, whether he was cocksure, elated, ('in the mountains') or depressed, negative, miserable ('in the tombs') he was always 'crying out', drawing attention to himself, and was his own worst enemy, 'cutting himself with stones'.

When he saw Jesus, he recognized him at once. Immediately he saw what spiritual health was. Such holiness filled him with unbearable remorse and all he wanted was to escape from it. 'What have I to do with thee?' he cried. Leave me alone. 'Torment me not.'

But Jesus simply asked him his name.

It was then the man gave his marvellous, inspired answer: 'My name is Legion, for we are many.'

Then, it seems, there was a sort of battle. Some of the 2000 people inside the man (the number is actually given) begged not to be sent out of him, while other 'devils' clamoured to be allowed, seeing what they were worth, to enter a herd of swine that were grazing nearby.

Then Jesus called the 'unclean spirit' out of the man and, so to say, cleansed him of his sinful life, gave leave to all those parts of him which had been destroying him to enter into the swine who promptly 'ran very violently down a steep place' and were destroyed.

The whole picture is there – not of some madman of a bygone age, but of each one of us today: self-centred, opinionated, wilful, changeable, always drawing attention to ourselves, always doing damage to the better parts of us by the kind of lives we lead, yet knowing, recognizing, that it is utterly against the kind of life we could live. Even when we are confronted by it, we turn aside, pretend not to notice, not daring to face the way we have wasted our opportunities.

It needs a Jesus with a look and a single command to change all that and make a man new.

So of course when all his neighbours who had known this man as a bad lot for years saw the sudden transformation, they were amazed and frightened of such power. For now the man was quiet, 'sitting', collected, still, 'clothed in his right mind', the way a man should be.

Naturally the man wanted to follow Jesus; but the Master told him to stay where he was among his neighbours and show them what life could be when inspired by compassion and love. 'And all men did marvel.'

12

Time

'Time in itself does not exist; there is only the totality of the results ensuing from all the cosmic phenomena present in the given place.'

The study of that 'something' that is always passing but never returns can help in the study of the theory of cosmoses which Gurdjieff proposes as basic to the understanding of the nature of life and the universe. In recent years the measurement of time has grown to be very important. Many who have not given it much thought, take time as a 'fact', as something built into life like speed or temperature – both of which, incidentally, are equally relative.

In fact the rate of passing of the phenomenon we call time is a convention based on a natural phenomenon thought of as more or less everlasting – the speed of the earth's rotation and its orbit round the sun. Taking the orbit as the unit for a year and its rotation as a day, the calendar takes note of the relatively slow passing of months and days, while the clock counts the hours, minutes, seconds. The arrangement does not fit exactly and periodic adjustments are necessary to keep the human time scale in step with the facts; but the whole thing is a convenience only and could equally well have been divided otherwise, say into a twenty-hour day and a fifty-hour minute; but, over the years, the present arrangements have been generally accepted and taken for granted. In fact time has become a god the whole world worships.

But it is only a measure of the rate of passing of events. It is because the period of the earth's orbit is fairly constant and the speed of its rotation steady that people have come to think of time as real, immovable, a fact. But were the earth's orbit to change or if (as ancient records show) its rate of rotation were to vary, then both calendar and timepiece would go out of step and the measurement of this passing 'something' would be in need of adjustment. The flow of time is constant only because the phenomena on which this flow is based is constant. Measuring it started as a sort of joke, an intellectual exercise. There were candle clocks, water clocks, sand clocks. For tens of thousands of years men had managed quite well without measuring time.

The flow of time is – or appears to be – constant, but it cannot be stopped, isolated or interfered with in any way. No man can save it or spend it or waste it, although the apparent rate of its passing can be related to personal states. If a man is caught, suspended in a period of anxiety or depression when nothing happens, time seems to drag slowly, tediously. There are no events to measure. On the other hand, if he is busily or actively engaged in something, hours go by in a flash. In either case what is really being measured is not time but the rate of passing of events.

A further property of time is that everything coming under its spell decays, falls into ruin and disintegrates. It is not directly destructive, like fire or an explosion; but it is the universal destroyer and its aim is to reduce everything to the bottom, to that prime source substance out of which the whole universe has been painstakingly built up. It is for this reason, to avoid this destruction that the Lord God, the universal Creator was constrained to bring the universe into existence. The living worlds, at every level, continually parry the destruction of time, building up, renewing and maintaining the universe.

Yet the destruction is necessary to life. There could be no life except under the threat of its extinction. How could it be always springing, new, were it not constantly destroyed? The very words 'birth' and 'death' imply destruction. Indeed time puts a razor edge on all experience. Comedy would be nothing if it was not set against tragedy. The sadness beyond comedy, the acceptance of all tragedy, is tempered, sharpened by the knowledge that it cannot stay.

Gurdjieff proposes a universe structured as it were concentrically, so that from the greatest to the smallest each world carries the lesser world within it. For example, the marvellous variety of the individual creations within Great Nature, are the cells in the body of that being we call organic life. And all these different varieties of beings – grasses, trees, birds, animals, insects, men – are themselves made up again of cells within their bodies. All of them, great or small, are complete, self-supporting 'worlds'. Each of them is a cosmos exactly similar in construction to those above and below it. The difference is only in scale. And at every scale, since every cell is alive, growth is possible, necessary to maintain the balance between God and time, the involutionary and evolutionary processes of life.

But the question of whether time is the same for each cosmos is another matter. Gurdjieff implies it is related to its place. Time appears to flow according to the rhythm of events in that particular cosmos. Just as earth time is linked to the planet's rotation, so time for the cells in our bodies may be linked to the heartbeat or the breathing. These rhythms, for cells which (to us) live a very short time, may be just as permanent and everlasting as the rotation of the world is to us.

Each cosmos has its own measure of the passing of time and, as cosmoses are related as zero to infinity, so is their time calculation. Only our time scale is real to us. The fact that the heartbeat may be the day and night of our bodily cells, or that sleeping and waking may be the cell's year, is impossible for us to understand. It is not our time scale.

A shot of morphine or a whiff of anaesthetic have an immediate effect on our bodies. The effect is almost instantaneous. But, to the body itself, with its infinitely slower time scale, that moment may last a decade. To man it seems a miracle how quickly the body reacts, how marvellously it adjusts, how perfectly it adapts to stress or accident. But maybe the body has plenty of time. It passes for the body at an infinitely slower rate.

At the opposite end of the scale the life of Great Nature appears everlasting. Nothing much seems to change over the millennia. But organic life is also a being. Beings need not be human beings, Nature, as a whole, as an entity, also has its life span, a time to develop, mature and die. On *its* time scale, the life of the beings that compose it (trees, birds, animals) must seem just as transient and ephemeral as the cells in the body of a man appear to him. He cares only for the whole. A man may burn up a million cells running a race. It does not matter: they will be replaced. So Great Nature can support war, famine, drought, pestilence. Life will regenerate. It is a momentary malaise, an indisposition, no more.

Beyond this it is impossible to do more than speculate about time. What can man understand about the lifespan of the earth, or of the sun? On his time scale both seem everlasting. All that this study shows is that each cosmos sees a fraction of some universal phenomenon and sees it as belonging to its life alone. To God, who sees the whole, time is subjective, personal to each cosmos; but to each separate cosmos it appears objective – the same for everybody.

13

The Golden Age

'Always guard against such perceptions as may soil the purity of your brains.'

Many thousands of years ago, it is said, humanity took a wrong turning. Its development began to change direction, no longer following the path along which the higher powers hoped it would develop. This change of direction, devastating and terrible in its effects, began when mankind started to be seduced by the attractions of the material world.

Hitherto all the activities of men, their government, their feasts, their skills and crafts, had been instinctively and consciously organized to feed and strengthen the inner life, the longing towards spiritual perfection. We can see this in the art and artefacts of ancient civilizations. They are all pointers or reminders that life is lived in the service of God.

Then came the change – a gradual, insidious change. Man began to be proud of his work, to value the material world for its own sake. Previously he had laboured for the glory of God, now he began to labour for his own glory. His work had been all service, now it began to be an end in itself. Men had painted Madonnas, then they painted their mistresses as Madonnas, then they painted their mistresses.

Today we have moved so far from this original vision of life that we cannot believe, or even imagine, how whole civilizations could have been so orientated. Today it is vaguely suspect to be interested in the religious life, then it was unthinkable to be anything else. Today the material world is all-important. For most of us, nothing else exists; in those days life was lived as an opportunity to make spiritual progress. It was a preparation, a testing for the life to come.

This is not to say that everyday life was pale and colourless, a sort of penitentiary. Clearly it was not. We can see from the carvings and frescoes of those days the evidence of great feasts and celebrations, of royal hunts and bitter wars, of a full and varied life. But what remains from all those days are not the palaces, but the temples. The memorials were of man's aspirations, not of his deeds.

Although we cannot possibly imagine what such a life was like, in some strange way we are attracted towards it; a vague dim nostalgia rises in us when we speak of the 'Golden Age'. Something, however vestigial, remains of those desires and manifestations that once rules men's lives. It feels safer and the more our frustrations and difficulties grow, the more the daily living of life seems empty and pointless – and who can deny that such feelings exist among us everywhere today – the more we yearn, somehow or other, someday or other, to find our way back to that path we have lost, to feel once again that, come what may, we are safe, we are on our way.

There was this time when life on earth was seen as a preparation, an ephemeral and transient affair because it was so hard and short, no more than a night's lodging on the long road of spiritual growth. All serious religions still preach more or less the same thing today and men who are reaching the end of the road often agree, seeing 'the little done, the undone vast'. But this is, in general, a latter-day discovery, not the self-evident fact it was to the ancient world. Today we are terrified of death and never speak of it; but in those days it was clear that although there might be some sort of entrance examination, heaven was the good man's destiny and the Lord was all-forgiving and generous in grace. Since no man can know what awaits him after death, the trust of the old beliefs seems more healthy and consoling than the bottomless pit of oblivion reserved for the unbelievers.

But besides this there was one enormous advantage this

Golden Age exercised over life today: there was no money.
Everything was barter, the exchange of goods. Man took
wine and gave wheat, took meat and gave oil. All trans-
actions were based on a fair exchange of actual goods. Values
were personal and approximate and the goods themselves
were consumable and could not be hoarded to make one man
rich at the expense of another. It is a very real thing to barter.
It touches the substance of life itself. It is human. When a
man needs a knife and is ready to exchange it for a pair of
boots, when he needs a donkey and is ready to swap it for an
umbrella, an exchange has taken place, quite different from
buying things at a shop.

Money, when it came, was of course a great convenience.
But it was not 'real'. It was just a token, a go-between. Only
gradually, as its use became more common, did it begin to
acquire *a value in itself*. Then it became the symbol of an
entirely new idea of reality, the material reality of *things*.
Possessions, ownership, wealth, became an aim in themselves, more rewarding, men said, because it was tangible and
bought status and ease. That all a man's life energy had been
spent on something he could not take with him was brushed
aside. The future was a question mark. Only what you could
see and hear, touch and taste, was real.

This basic reversal of values gained ground until today it
has swamped everything else. This is why it is so hard for all
those who seek to live by the old values. From childhood we
have been taught to think of everything in material terms. Yet
all this belongs to the impermanent aspect of life, but we have
been conditioned so thoroughly that nobody sees it, nobody
cares. The old masters taught that the experiences and suffer-
ings of life were a means by which we could, if we met them
rightly, gain spiritual merit and, so to speak, grow our souls.
But all this, which is our birthright, we have, like Cain,
bartered for a mess of potage.

This excursion into prehistory, to the days of the Golden Age,
is all very well; but some may say: 'What's the good of
delving into all this? It doesn't exist any more. Our business is

with our own lives, today, now. Anything else is a waste of time.'

But do you remember that old conundrum: if you came to a big road junction in a strange country and found the signpost had been blown down in a gale, how could you set it up again to be sure you continued in the right direction? The answer is you couldn't – unless you knew where you had come from. If you set up that arm right, all the rest would fall into place.

Before we can move in any direction, we must know where we are and where we have come from. We must try, as far as possible, to see our situation, to see how we have gradually and increasingly put all our emphasis on the material side of life at the expense of the spiritual and how this reversal has led us to see reality upside down. And just as our eyes really receive the images of the outside world reversed and we have learned since birth to compensate for this so thoroughly we can't believe anything else, so believing only in the outside world is fundamental, axiomatic. How could we live in any other way? The distortion is complete. The unreal has become the real.

I say all this, but I know you can't believe it. You don't see how you can live in any other way. Yes, it takes time, struggle and candid self-examination to even begin to accept that it would be possible to go through life less deeply attached to the material side of it, living by an inner set of values, not by the quicksand of man-made morality which changes as quickly and unpredictably as the weather.

These social values, by which most of us are ruled all our lives, are really a house of cards. They are continually changing, falling down and having to be cobbled together, bodged, repaired and tarted up to suit the changing kaleidoscope of human behaviour. What can we find permanent in them? What is there in them to live by? And because there is nothing, we grow a sort of armour, a thick hide of 'don't know and don't care', put our heads down and plug on to nowhere. And if anyone comes along and says: 'Look, you're putting the cart before the horse', we are up in arms at once: 'Don't you come adding to all my difficulties and frustrations with a lot of new ideas. Don't ask me to face more complications.'

And that is really where we stand. And there really is no hope until we begin to admit that the outside world is not everything and that we all have within us a child, an undeveloped creature we keep in the dark, but which could, if we would only let it, grow and mature and in growing teach us to find a new pride in ourselves, a new hope, a new certainty for the future.

To come to that blessed moment is to escape from the dreary hopelessness in which we are trapped and that you may reach it is the hope to take with you.

14

Eternal Recurrence

'If a man is changing every minute, if there is nothing in him that can withstand external influences, it means there is nothing in him that can withstand death. If a man develops permanent 'I' that can survive a change in external conditions, it can survive the death of the physical body.'

I suppose it is natural that when a man gets to the end of one life, he should contemplate his chances of starting another one.

Death, like the sun, is something no one can look at for long. Indeed the life force does not wish us to do so, for that might weaken the creative urge on which the whole future depends. We cannot face our own extinction. It is a good thing, for in any case we cannot escape it and can have no idea whatever of what lies beyond it.

Nevertheless down the centuries, wherever men and women have formed societies they have soon started to worry at this unanswerable question: is there an afterlife and, if so, what must they do to ensure it? Not for nothing is this riddle deeply embedded in the consciousness of the race, for the very fact that it cannot be answered forces us into a continual evaluation of the living of life. For some unaccountable reason, we aspire to be other than we are and this aspiration becomes a sort of yardstick against which to measure our deeds and attitudes and so finally to assess whether – in our own opinion of course – we are worthy to 'go to heaven' or not.

But consider for a moment what would be the effect of knowing, *for certain*, that there was an afterlife, and the price to be paid for it. What incentive would there be for a man to be better, if he knew he had already piled up enough pluses to ensure his angelic future? The very fact that he does not know keeps him striving. Equally the man who was convinced he had failed miserably would soon cease to continue – if he had ever started – to make any efforts at all. Nobody knows how he has done in the divine exam.

An almost exact parallel is given to the student of Zen Buddhism when, at a certain point in his work, he is given an unanswerable question, called a koan, to solve. Perhaps the most famous of such questions is: 'What is the sound of one hand clapping?' He cannot find the answer. Indeed there is no answer. But in doggedly keeping the question before him, sometimes for months or years, the moment comes when a totally new level of understanding floods in on him, called enlightenment. The question of death and the afterlife is just such a koan to all of us. Pondering it and keeping it before us can lead us towards a kind of life we could not possibly live without.

Whatever this unknown future may hold, there are broadly speaking two main theories about it. One is the supposition that there is somewhere *another life* in which we, retaining all our individual functions, continue to live. The other is the theory that we return, or are reincarnated in *this life*, here on earth and endlessly repeat ourselves in a sort of immortal treadmill.

We might examine these two alternatives.

If there is one fact of which we are all certain it is that no dead creature comes back to life. The withering of all things at the hand of time is irreversible. So the concept of resurrection runs contrary to everything we know and that is why it is so difficult to believe.

The idea of some future life in which all wrongs are redressed and all sorrows swept away has persisted down the ages. But when we begin to enquire where this future life is lived and what its purpose is, the replies are apt to be evasive and euphoric. It will not stand up to examination. Today on a point so vital to all of us, we cannot be content with fairy tales.

The resurrection of Jesus Christ has given an immense impetus to these ideas and the Church has magnified a single miraculous occurrence of one superman into a generality which has been somehow stretched as if it were open to all of us. There is nothing in the Gospels to suggest that such an idea was part of the teaching of Jesus. It has been grafted onto the faith, hallowed by tradition and is so reassuring that nobody questions it.

There are many instances on the fringes of religion where there were men who had acquired special powers and had been able to materialize a second self, exactly imitating the original, and cause this to appear, sometimes at great distances, to take part in some teaching or ritual. There are other magical formulae by which a group of disciples, working in a special way, are able to rematerialize a teacher who has recently died and bring him back for a short time in order that he may impart to them some important truth which sudden death or accident has prevented being revealed in his life. But all such things are special possibilities open to the very few. They in no way justify a general belief in the resurrection of the body and a life everlasting being lived in it.

But still the idea of life everlasting crops up in another form when we try to discover what the essence of life is. Where does it reside? What are its attributes? You remember the old riddle: 'Does life reside in the leg? No, for if you cut it off, life continues.' Similarly with sight, speech or hearing: remove them, still life continues. Life does not reside in any function. Then where does it reside – what is it?

So the idea begins to emerge that life, whatever it is, is different, separate, from the creature in which it resides, a sort of power house, or spark, or nuclear element which continually radiates something which inspires all functioning to take place. But, like radio sets, are we battery charged or mains operated? Is our life force individual, slowly running

down with use, or is it continually recharged from some
general power house? Have we a divine component, immortal,
inexhaustible, a piece of God? Fascinating questions!

The other belief – widely held – of our prospects for a future
life is a theory generally known as reincarnation. It proposes
that some essential or immortal part is able to withstand the
shock of death and, after an interval, not clearly defined, is
somehow able to return to earth in another body.

As I have already said we cannot face our own extinction;
but if we try, for a moment, to look at it impartially, the
question immediately arises: 'Why should I continue? What
is there so important or valuable about me that I am justified
in believing that I must not be lost?' Obviously nothing.
Certain exceptional people have lived, great teachers, artists,
scientists, who have made splendid contributions to the
fabric of life; but they could not go on making them. They
come to the end of themselves. The vein is worked out;
another is necessary.

So the question arises: if something is reincarnated, what is
it? Personally, I find I cannot believe in the persistence of
personality, in all the quirks and foibles, pleasant and unpleasant, that manifest in me daily. All this is the froth on the
beer. Underneath lies what I think of as the essential me, the
core of my life and, although I am not too familiar with it, I
feel it to be more genuine than the daily suits of clothes I am
always changing. Is this the part that can return?

Well, if all living creatures are set in motion by some divine
spark we called the life force, is this energy parcelled out into
individual charges, each having a separate entity? Or, to put
it another way, do the drops of water splashed out of the
bucket remain separate drops when they are back in the
bucket? That is the question. If you believe that they do, then
your survival, your immortality, as a personal entity is assured.
If you do not, then you are forced to the conclusion that life is
transient, ephemeral and if anything does continue to exist it
is quite different in form and possibility from anything we
can imagine.

Gurdjieff insists, as always, on quality. If we have lived superficial, empty, selfish lives, what is there to survive death? If we have struggled and suffered maybe some immortal part may return to undergo further refinement – but nothing is guaranteed. If we are fortunate this purification may continue through many lives until we are finally freed to be a help to our Creator 'in an enlarging world' as he puts it.

God helps us because He needs us as much as we need Him. That is the important idea. So a new concept of immortality arises, in which we can be *of use*, in which there is the possibility of our own spiritual development, our own *growth* – and that is infinitely more positive and hopeful than any other answer to this riddle that I know.

Finally, since we do not and cannot know the answer, we must fall back on 'Thy will be done', that is on faith – which is trust – and that is perhaps the most difficult of all.

15

Right Attitude

'A man can take everything in such a personal way as if everything in the world had been specially arranged to give him pleasure or to cause him inconvenience or unpleasantness.'

There is an attitude to life of which we never speak. We keep it a secret because we know it is a fake. Yet it plays a very important part in everyday life. It is the act we put on to impress people, to make them think we are smarter, more intelligent, richer than we are. In the teaching that I follow it is called considering – inner considering – a process, practically continuous, which runs through our lives and by which, inside, we are always considering the effect we are having on others.

We are on a bus, say, in company with a lot of people we do not know, have never seen before and probably will never see again. What they think of us, what we think of them, is utterly unimportant and yet a part of us keeps up a continuous running commentary: 'Is my tie straight? Do I need more powder? How do I look? What is that man thinking of me? If I cross my feet nobody will notice my stocking is laddered. I must keep my frayed cuff out of sight.'

Trivial matters, yet, if we look, they light up our abject slavery to the opinions of others, a slavery to the idea of how we want others to see us and a ball and chain to all our hopes of freedom. And this is not only personal, individual, it applies just as forcefully to political parties seeking votes, to societies canvassing for members, to nations justifying aggression. It is the most pervasive form of egoism. The world, its opinions, morals, successes, failures, are all master-minded by inner considering.

Its opposite, outer considering, in which all the focus, all the effort is directed to the other and the self is merely a servant, is an ideal to be aimed at, an alternative almost beyond us because the habit of referring everything to the self is so ingrained, so much part of our behaviour patterns, we really do not know how to reverse it. But perhaps the first step towards freeing ourselves from our slavery is to see the extent of it.

I once knew a man who saw his slavery quite clearly and found an original way of fighting it. He was a middle-aged man, but he bought a bright red schoolboy's peaked cap and put it on his head. He wore it to the office, he wore it in the evening. Wherever he went he wore this conspicuous, ridiculous hat. Of course it attracted a lot of attention. Everyone thought he was a nut.

And all the time his work was not to give way to this inner considering of other people's opinions, to their laughter, their superiority, their contempt. It faced him with his enemy, his slavery to life. Then one day, some months later, I saw him again hatless, as he had been before. The cap had been thrown away. The lesson had been learned.

This desperate need to pretend we are more than we are traps us in a perpetual lie. We may have some spectacular talent or ability but, taken as a whole, few of us can claim to be genuinely superior people. We can't admit it, of course. But to a lesser or greater degree, all of us consider inwardly. We are slaves to this lie and we cannot escape it.

And the devil of it is we are all doing it to each other. If you think for a minute what this means, you will see it adds up to a nightmare situation. Our whole lives, and that of society, are shot through with – more, fundamentally based on – falsehood. How can we hope for good relations with other people, to live honourably and truthfully, in such a gigantic cover up?

But, mercifully for our peace of mind, this attitude is so deeply ingrained in us it seems the normal, natural way to behave. It is not until we begin to look a little more closely that we see what Gurdjieff calls 'the terror of the situation'. What is it sets up this attitude? Why do we feel bound to impress, to mount this façade of appearances all day and every day? Could it be that we look on all so-called friendly relationships as being with an adversary, an enemy, us against them? Am I so unsure of myself that I must assert myself? I do it in a hundred ways, not only by plain aggression but by showing off, by being clever, by using my charm – anything to be superior, to fake my one-upmanship. What a far cry it is from the honest, friendly life we like to think we lead! Think this over and you will realize it is impossible to imagine what the world would be like if it were free from inner considering.

When I was at boarding school, we used to go to church on Sundays, morning and evening. I don't remember much about it except the Athanasian Creed, which we all chanted aloud. There was one phrase in it that got my hackles up: 'There is no health in us.' I refused to say it. I didn't believe it. It wasn't true. I was full of life, of health, why should I lie? Sunday after Sunday, as we came to it, I shut up and listened to the other chaps droning away without thinking what they were saying.

But today I am not so sure. There is a way we are all inoculated from childhood to live this false, unhealthy life.

Is it really me against the world? What am I defending? What am I proving? Why can I not be content to be full of contradictions and prejudices, of hates and loves, as everybody else is? I readily see the defects in others, but I somehow imagine – and it's really a big laugh – that I can hide my own! Why is there this deep fear in all of us, the fear of being seen for what we are?

There was once a great pharaoh in ancient Egypt who began all his proclamations: 'I, the King, living in truth'. He was called a heretic, despised and rejected; but in that one phrase he set fire to the aspirations of mankind. How can we learn to live in truth?

It is not until we begin to face up to our simple everyday behaviour that we see how far we are from living that good life which, when we are fired with enthusiasm and hope, seems just around the corner. But the fact is that, having been conditioned since childhood to cheat and fake and lie without noticing it, we carry a heavy burden. Only perhaps in old age, when we no longer give a damn what people think, can we began to put the burden down because we see how feeble and ridiculous all our posturing is.

How can we begin to face this problem in everyday life? It all comes back to the central theme of every serious religion – that of being awake, being present to what is going on around us. If we are quick we can catch our lies, putting on our act, being superior to our friends and, in a hundred ways, attempting to hoodwink others into thinking we are wonderful people.

But if we refer all this swaggering, this bravado, to another part of ourselves – our inner guardian or judge – who is not deceived and tells us in a quiet but quite unequivocal way that all this is false, we may begin to face things as they are – which is the beginning of all relationships.

It is by seeing all this going on, by catching ourselves in the act, so to speak, that we become less liable to do it. It isn't easy, but, little by little, we begin to hate the false and to see that another simpler kind of life would be possible, could we but rid ourselves of this load of lies we struggle under.

We are all carrying a heavy burden and, as we see it, it becomes, or seems to become, heavier. But, in fact, like all the trials and tribulations of this life, it is perfectly adjusted to our strength. Too much will never be put upon us. If the weight becomes too great, God comes to our aid to spare us what is too much for us to carry.

You remember the Sufi story of the man who found his cross too heavy? He went to the shop where crosses were made and said to the maker of crosses, 'This cross is much too heavy for me. Could I change it?'

'Sure,' replied the cross maker, 'help yourself.' So the man went round the place trying on all sorts of crosses. Some were

16

The Card Index

'There are ... in their brains what are called 'bobbin-candelnosts', that is to say, something that gives such brains or localizations a definite quantity of possible associations or experiencings.'

The other day I received a letter. I didn't know the writing, the postmark was unfamiliar, but as soon as I saw the signature, I remembered: someone I hadn't seen for twenty years! A whole cluster of memories surfaced: how he had looked then, the tone of his voice, his interests, his sense of humour, and so on and so on.

This is a very common experience. We have all had it. But the miracle of it we take for granted – how, given the right stimulus, we can enter a particular file in our card index – our memory – recorded perhaps half a century before, and find there all the details of the experience, together with attendant circumstances, giving a complete picture of a life we once lived, of the way we were then.

This ability to recall varies widely from person to person. It also varies with our state, our health, our age, our interest; but we all have it. Indeed life would be impossible without memory. Plays and books have been written to illustrate the theme – how people can go mad when they cannot remember who they are, what has happened to them. We all stand on a pedestal of memory.

The master files of our past are fairly easy to enter; but grouped round them in the shadows are many we cannot open at all. What was that chap's name? Who wrote that tune? That view's familiar, but I can't place it. Associations are boundless, endless, unpredictable; but there is one very important fact about all memory, vital to an understanding of its place and purpose: it is none of it *new*. It's all old stuff – on file.

These files are a record of our past. Everything is recorded. All our impressions, what we have seen or heard, what we have read or thought, our opinions, experiences, loves, fears, everything is there – whether we can reach it or not. Nothing is lost. But we have a trick of rearranging this memory store in new ways and so creating fairy tales, fantasies, rehashing what happened into new patterns. It's something like a kaleidoscope, the coloured beads change their picture if we turn the tube. That is how we make our dreams.

So we all stand at every moment before this enormous background of our collected impressions, living our way of life. Because of this way we live, very little is really seen, really new. It all slips into our files almost unnoticed, to become part of our associations.

The thought I want to leave with you is this: association is not thought. It is just browsing among our files. But life is not the contemplation of dead things. Real thought, the faculty for which our heads were designed, is quite different, quite new.

Association and thought are quite different things. Association – which we generally call thought – is the putting together of experiences and ideas that are already there, on file, in our heads, and sometimes making new patterns out of the old bricks. Thought, on the other hand, is something brand new. It comes like a lightning flash, a revelation. Thought is something you have never thought before.

We are all familiar – though perhaps only rarely – with the excitement of being struck by a new idea. It is a surprise, something quite different from the ordinary progressive thinking we are used to – like a goods train shunting, each truck budging the one ahead – the way we normally work out our problems. Thought is something totally different, in a different class. A brand new thought leaps, fully grown, into the mind. Our immediate reaction is one of wonder. 'Of course! Why didn't I think of it before!' The effect is so striking that we often call it a 'revelation', a moment of inspiration or the answer to a prayer; but in fact it is only the active part of our head working as it was meant to work.

Our question of course is: 'Why can't this happen more often? Why do I so rarely get the answer?' If we try to look at these moments of real thought more closely, we see that what they really are is a deeper understanding of the circumstances. They penetrate beyond the normal, the logical, to reach the heart of the matter. It is as if they came from a different level.

And this indeed is what it is. Our memory files are stored in a huge underground catacomb. Miles and miles of dark twisty, narrow passages house these archives, many of which are never visited. The files are deep in dust, the light doesn't work and, as we get older, big areas of our filing system are quite inaccessible to us. Our memory plays tricks with us, we say. The place is dark. We have forgotten.

Thought isn't in the basement, it's on the ground floor in the light of day and sometimes even on the upper floors where the unknown sacred part of us lives. But we're so used to the basement, the daylight dazzles us.

To change the metaphor, we can think we have a sort of receptionist at the doorway of our lives, who has taken on the job of answering all enquiries. The directors – our real thoughts and feelings – are shut away in their offices and this 'frontman' is employed to use the card index. He is frightfully slick at it. He always has an answer, even if it's quite untrue and he dishes out these lies and insincerities all day long. Our 'frontman' cuts us off from our neighbour – for he too, remember, has his 'frontman'. This is one of the reasons we so often fail to make relations with people.

So here I am with my card index. I catch myself in conversation – even with intimate friends – knowing perfectly well my 'frontman' is on the job. This isn't what I really think, really feel. It's a sort of smoke screen I put up to *hide* what I think and feel. Why must I do it – hide what I really am? Because all my life I have been educated to an idea of how I want to be seen and now I desperately keep up the façade. So the real me is smothered, deeper and deeper.

And the joke is that the people I talk to know this just as well as I do. Because they are doing the same thing! Our 'frontman', the 'barker' as he is sometimes called, is a magician the way he juggles with my memory files, but most of it adds up to nothing. We spend hours and hours in our all-too-short lives in futile and unnecessary conversation.

Back of all this is the real part of us that thinks and feels and has its own patterns and rhythms. But it's a prisoner. It can't get past the 'barker'. Indeed it's sometimes as if this real self of ours was starved or retarded. We don't know *what* we think or feel. We're tongue-tied if we try, it's so unusual! Yet this is the real us, the only part which, if we give it a chance, can grow and blossom. How can we expect any relationship if it's only my dummy speaking to your dummy? Or any relationship with ourselves for that matter. Watch people's expressions passing in the street, locked into solitary confinement with their dreams. We are all the same.

I was going to say there's nothing to be done about this. This is how the world is, how we are. But that would not be true. There is something to be done, a little, very big, thing: *to see it; I am like this*!

Nearly all my life is a string of lies and insincerities and it's all become so usual, such a deep habit, I don't even notice it.

You know we all look for heroics in religion – the noble gesture, the great renunciation, the blinding insight – but it's very rarely like that. An aim within my reach is to make a penny into two pence, to struggle, day by day, to see myself as I am.

It is a task within the reach of all of us and from it will come wonderful things: compassion for your neighbour, for he is in the same plight as you – blind, hopeless, locked in. Seeing your dilemma, you see all men's.

What a revelation to grow from such a simple thing: just to look in, instead of looking out, for the real wonders, believe me, are inside, not outside.

17

Jacob's Ladder

'Blessed is he that hath a soul and blessed is he that hath none, but grief and sorrow are to him that hath in himself its making.'

'**H**ow do you think you look?' said my wife to me the other day, having completed her new-found skill of cutting my hair. The venerable ruin that represents my 93 years of commerce with this wicked world looked back at me from the glass. 'Lovely!' I said. 'I look absolutely smashing.'

We laughed together; but underneath the laughter came an awkward little twinge I hardly bothered to look at I took it so much for granted. I *did* think, not perhaps that I was absolutely smashing, but that I was OK, not so bad considering. I suddenly saw all that smoke screen of false modesty and self-deprecation we put up to conceal the fact that, privately, we really *do* think we're the elephant's pyjamas.

As a matter of fact we don't think about it at all. We take it so absolutely for granted. All of us – prime minister to tramp, field marshall to terrorist, tycoon to beggar – we are all convinced we occupy the centre of a stage in which everything depends on us, is referred to us, takes orders from us. In our private world we are all kings and queens.

Now, of course, with another part of ourselves we know that's nonsense. We are perfectly well aware that some people may dislike us or disagree with us, think us obstinate or stupid; but whatever the situation, whether we're rebuffed or shouted down, refused or ignored, inside there's a still small voice which won't take no for an answer, which insists – and finds a hundred reasons to prove it – that we are right and the world wrong. I am justified. I am never defeated.

You may feel I'm labouring this a bit. Why not say we're all pig-headed egoists and leave it at that? Why not indeed? There is a point of view from which it is absolutely right for us to be pig-headed egoists. We are. We must be. To keep our place in the world we must look after number one. It's not selfish, it's natural. After all Nature is our nurse, our teacher and what does she do? Watch a cat stalking a bird or a wasp attacking a spider. In the marvellous ecology of Nature everything lives on everything else. Somebody dies for somebody else to live. Incredible complications give every creature a defence against the enemy that lives to feed on it. The whole thing is based on our overwhelming instinct to survive, on the force and pre-eminence of egoism.

You see the dilemma? This marvellous world with all its majesty and beauty must be the work of a divine Creator. Yet in close-up it is a jungle, a relentless struggle for survival. So the same God that gave us the instincts to kill, gave us also the commandment to deny the self, renounce the world, love our enemies and live for our neighbours.

It is an impasse. How can we face such a universal question?

One side of us insists on its right to be full-blooded egoist and another has an urge, an impulse, to live quite another sort of life in which egoism has no part.

We are doomed, it seems, to a life of contradiction. We are two-natured, 'half God and half brute', as Masefield put it. We live in two worlds. And this dual nature is our birthright, our place as human beings in the miraculous jigsaw of the natural world in which we live. Only we humans are blessed and cursed with this dichotomy, the ability to question, to reason, to compare abstracts. In our world we are free to choose, to face the eternal problems of right and wrong, good and evil. This brings us slowly to the conviction that there is a direction which we ought to follow, to the recognition of responsibility, of remorse, of sin.

All these problems, these difficulties are, so to speak, piled on top of our animal nature which still has its rights – to eat, to procreate, to make a place for itself. So there is always a balance to be struck, a harmony to be found, between what are sometimes called our lower and higher natures. So we've got well nigh insoluble problems.

Does it matter? Perhaps they are not meant to be solved, only to be struggled with. Perhaps this earth is specifically designed to be a place of struggle, of conflict, of doubt – to see what we can make of it. If we could arrive at a destination in life and put our feet up, we should be bored stiff in ten minutes, with nothing to overcome, nothing to fight. Many pictures have been painted of heaven; but they have only one thing in common – they are out of reach. And that is as it should be.

Now there are certainly plenty of people who don't want to tangle with these questions at all, who say that 'topside up is right side up' and keep their nose pretty close to the ground. But there are others who recognize a possibility that their centre of gravity could lie in the growth of their inner life, and who steadfastly and wholeheartedly work towards it.

Perhaps life on earth is this very purgatory we have often read about, a place of purification. How do you purify things? You wash them, purge them and put them through the fire. It takes a long time to produce one perfect thing, as every craftsman knows.

So the question is how to learn this craft of life?

We are born all possibilities with nothing lived; we die with a life lived and no more possibilities. Our possibilities lie in the living, in the struggle, in what we make of life. Many people see this in purely practical terms – fame, wealth, position and so on. They are not in the least concerned with any 'inner' life. It never occurs to them that they have one even. These are the people whom Gurdjieff refers to as being happy because they have no soul – 'Let us eat, drink and be merry, for tomorrow we die.' At the other end of the scale are those who by luck and effort have tasted quite another sort of

life. There are very few of them. A million acorns fall from
the oak, but maybe only one becomes a tree. We are not
concerned with either of these categories. They are perfectly
all right as they are. Our business is with the middle ground.
That is, with you and me.

We have somehow wakened up to the realization that we
are not all of a piece. We are not as we could be, should be.
We see our contradictions. And we have somehow also become aware that there is a part of us, very vague, very hard to
define, which wants things to grow, to be different, which
aspires to a nobler, richer and, as the Bible puts it, more
righteous life. We have a soul in the making.

The trouble is we are so inconsistent. At one moment
nothing but the growth of our spiritual life interests us. Our
whole being points towards it. At the next we get so involved
in looking at the television or cooking the supper that we
completely forget there is such a thing as the inner life. This
part of us has never heard of it. How do we bring these two
parts together?

It is the eternal problem of the religious life. The first thing
is to see it, accept it. I am like that. This is how it is. I accept
the challenge. The battle is on. Soon will follow the realization that I simply don't know how to go forward. I am lost
in a strange country and I need help. Then comes the careful,
painstaking search for someone who knows and is willing
and able to give me the help I need.

Many never find it, perhaps because they give up. They
don't want it enough, maybe, or are not yet ready for the
struggle, sometimes up, sometimes down, never at rest. But
that's how it is and must be.

Do you remember Jacob and that wonderful dream he had
of a ladder set between earth and heaven and the angels going
up and down on it? Well, there we are! There is a picture of
the entire human condition. We are climbing a ladder and,
because we can't make up our minds, going up and down on
it.

Don't ask me why we should climb ladders at all. We must
because we can.

18

Choosing a Path

'The highest aim and sense in human life is the striving to obtain the welfare of one's neighbour.'

In these tumultuous days through which we are living there seems to be no aspect of human activity, personal or collective, that escapes scrutiny. No wonder we yearn for the stability and security of the past faced with this collective urge to destroy everything that has gone before, to revel in the prospect of chaos.

But at the same time this aimless, mindless slide towards anarchy stimulates many to question more seriously. In their personal lives, where do they stand? What, if anything, do they believe in, not only in the more obvious practical area of politics, economics or daily life but also in that more subtle world of hidden values on which, we are beginning to suspect, everything else depends? After all, if a man is looking for better relationships, better citizenship, he soon sees they must rest squarely on the personal attitude of the citizen, in what we call his morality. And his morality in turn rests squarely on some code of belief. Sometimes while professing the belief, he denies the source. That does not matter. What matters is that we should see there can be no return to a less negative destructive state without the active participation of conscience in our daily lives.

I do not mean that rootless, time-serving conscience shaped by fashion or convention which varies from country to country and class to class. I mean the changeless, deep-flowing conscience of the Ten Commandments and the Sermon on the Mount, which sets an everlasting yardstick of values and finds a deep response hidden within us.

However today there is a tendency to repudiate the mainstream of religious teaching in favour of a wide variety of cults, sects or movements which, because of their novelty or of their simplistic presentation seem to offer quick, easy answers to people who are looking for something but don't quite know what it is. Sometimes these 'novelties' have real roots and a real new message of help and hope, sometimes they are old beliefs revitalized by the leadership of remarkable men. Sometimes the leaders may be spurious charlatans, conning their followers into worshipping them for the sake of power or money.

For those to whom this problem is serious because they are themselves searching for a valid way to live their lives, we could examine what to look for – and what to avoid – in this search.

People who are searching for something are quite different from those who are not. The searchers are those restless, dissatisfied ones who have made the big step forward of seeing something about themselves. They have noticed a gap between capacity and performance, between what they are and what, in some ill-defined way, they feel they could be.

This beginning to see yourself is a very big step. It divides you at once from all those perfectly good but unreflective people who never tangle with this sort of thing at all.

Neither do we who have seen it, most of the time. Only now and then does something remind us, wake up inside us to see ourselves and our situation more clearly, more vividly than usual. These wakings are quite special. We can't predict them or make them happen, yet when they do they somehow seem to join us to another quality of life.

It is this sort of experience – which many of you will recognize – which begins to turn our attention to a whole range of questions, which differ as much as we differ. It may lead us towards religion or philosophy, to sociology, to medicine or to science. Whatever it is, as a result we begin to look more deeply into life. Of course the impulse may fade or be smothered by the pressures of life; but if the questions go deep enough they are not so easily forgotten and they lead us inevitably to 'What am I? What is the sense and aim of my existence?' When you begin to ask these sorts of questions it may be said your search is serious.

But at this point something quite strange can happen. These thoughts and feelings have become very important to you; but they are very personal, very private, and you shrink from speaking about them from fear of exposing yourself to criticism or ridicule. So the thing gets bottled up inside you, a sort of dreadful secret you must always carry, but can never talk about for fear of giving yourself away.

But, curiously enough, this may turn out not to be a bad thing, for it means the questions go on churning round inside you and may easily lead you to the crux of the matter. I know nothing, I understand nothing. My life is slipping away day by day, month by month, year by year in a sort of dream, a fantasy. I don't control it; it controls me. It doesn't make sense. Answers there must be, but who knows them? How can I find them?

When it gets to that point, something can happen for you.

Very often there seems to be an awful lot of luck in the way we take the big decisions in our lives. We talk of fate or the long arm of coincidence; but whatever it is, momentous decisions seem to arise from trivia. Napoleon is supposed to have lost the battle of Waterloo because he had a bad cold in the head.

So it is pretty certain that in this search of yours to make sense of your life, however shy or tentative your desire for help, somehow or other, sooner or later, quite casually, through reading a book or chatting with a friend or perhaps some chance encounter, suddenly a possibility will open. It is a most important moment, perhaps the most important in your life, and if you are wise you will have all your antennae out. Some people are naïve and trusting in the way they commit themselves to the unknown. Others have a built-in caution and are slower to enthuse. Some miss all their opportunities by being too timid to decide about anything. You bring yourself to this encounter. So watch it!

There are three sorts of possibilities you may fall in with. The most numerous are all those cults, sects and movements which may broadly be called eccentric. They will tell you the only true 'way' lies in diet or drugs, in astrology or hypnosis. Some are secret societies with very strict rules, others are communes where everything is shared, from beds to boots. They are all very plausible but not always what they seem. Remember the shoot-out in Wako? If you are serious and cautious you will be able to sidestep this category.

The second sort of encounter you may make is more subtle. It is the possibility of working with a teacher who has, at some time or other, been connected with a real centre, but who has broken away from it and set up on his own. He knows something, but it is not enough. Often he has a lot of charisma mixed with egoism; but somehow, in the end, his work is sterile. It doesn't lead anywhere. You have asked for bread and are given a stone. To follow this line may not do you much harm, but it can end in disillusion.

If you are persistent you may meet and reject both these categories before you fall in with the third and join the preparatory school that has links going down to the taproots of the everlasting truths. They are not easy to find. They don't advertise. But if you are needy – and lucky – you will get there.

Don't be put off by labels. There is only one prime source and, in the end, all teachings teach the same truths. Choose the path that suits you. Christian, Jew, Sufi, Buddhist, Hindu or Gurdjieff, their paths are different, but the aim is the same – to seek the perfecting and purification of the self.

When you have got to this point, you have reached the end of your search – but it is only the beginning.

19

Operation Hope

'Thanks to this abnormal hope of theirs a very very singular and most strange disease, with a property of evolving, arose and exists among them even until now, a disease called – Tomorrow.'

I often think that not the least remarkable thing about Churchill's life was the manner in which, towards the end of it, he planned the final ceremonies by which his death should be commemorated. To be objective and yet so practical as to allow the living mind to contemplate the rituals following its own end is a mark of greatness it is not given many of us to reach. He called the plan, I believe, 'Operation Hope Not', and the terrible finality of the phrase started me thinking about the enormous part hope plays in all our lives.

Hope colours almost everything we do and say. We hope it will be fine tomorrow or that our latest business deal will come off. We hope our health will improve or that our relations with family or friends will get better. We hope that our horse will win or we shan't catch a cold. We hope, in short, for a happy outcome to our affairs and, in a very strange way, however often our hopes are dashed, we seem able to adjust them, change their focus, and so manage to maintain a buoyancy, a resilience, without which, it seems, we should find it almost impossible to go on living. If you think about it for a moment it's impossible not to be impressed at the way in which unfortunate people, faced by disaster after disaster, still find this extraordinary capacity to hope.

But there is something about hope we all take for granted and that is the way it's always attached to our desires. We always hope *in* something. Hope is a pair of rose-coloured spectacles through which we view our future. It is the sort of bias we give to our possibilities, the sugar icing we put on our intentions, our wishes, our plans. And, of course, it is always in the future. You cannot hope in yesterday.

But there is another quality of hope which is not attached to all the things we do and say, but to a deeper, less obvious part of us, a part which I would call our essence, which hopes for the good for the good's sake. It is a part which is, so to speak, buried, but yet might come alive and grow. It is the sort of hope which is almost a prayer.

So the question arises: 'Are there hopes beyond my own desires, my own egoism? Have I — deeply hidden, of course — real needs for which I could legitimately, and not selfishly, hope? Is there, in fact, a genuine Operation Hope beyond Churchill's Operation Hope Not?'

We all have a deeply buried part of us with quite different needs and hopes from our personalities, the part which, so to speak, lives our lives for us. I called this part the essence.

Essence is our birthright, born into life with us, our budding set of possibilities, our genetic heredity. Personality, on the other hand, does not come from the inside, the source of life, but is impressed onto us by the influences around us. We start, if you like, as a clean sheet of paper on which those around us begin to write. Mothers write, fathers write, brothers, sisters, friends, relations, all write. And all they say is faithfully recorded in our thoughts, feelings and habits in a very complex way. They are not our own, but once we have received them, we store them, rearrange them in the memory and subsequently bring them out *as if they were our own*.

If we happen to be surrounded by loving parents and friends, we shall record those kinds of impressions. If we are subject to unhappy, discontented or violent people, we shall inevitably be influenced by that kind of life. Of course circumstances alter cases. There may be something in our genetic inheritance so powerful it eclipses everything else; but, in general, the personality we emerge with at maturity is compounded of an extremely complicated set of impressions recorded in our personal, private computers.

This mish-mash of second-hand material, of which we cannot remember one hundredth part, is what we face life with. Often these two, essence and personality, have nothing in common. Indeed they may be in violent conflict. We often hear of people whose lives have become so painful to them that they rebel, have breakdowns and only recover when they reach something totally different. Their smothered essence has finally refused to allow the dressed-up dummy of their personality to run their lives, to ruin what they really are.

Now do you begin to see how hope comes into all this? For we have attached our hopes to our personalities, to the part of us that is not really ours. Daily life has swamped, squashed, the only part that can genuinely hope – and it is a life sentence.

So what is to be done in such a desperate situation?

Had we been rightly brought up, properly educated, these two parts of ourselves, essence and personality, would have been harmonized, our outer and inner lives brought into relation with each other. Then our priorities would be saner, our values clearer and there would be genuine objective hope for all of us.

Sometimes when people begin to see this basic division in themselves, they want to condemn personality altogether, because it is a fraud, a fake, and they jump to the conclusion that if they could live solely in essence, they would be living in truth and the problem would be solved. But we cannot do this. We are two-natured and we cannot throw away our personalities any more than we can go about daily life in the nude. We need our clothes to be able to carry on our outer life, we need our essence to foster the development of our inner life. This conflict is our birthright. It is also our cross. Life on earth is – and is meant to be – struggle: struggle between what I do and what I am.

Where are we in all this today? We have forgotten every-thing but our clothes. We live for appearances, for material things. But it doesn't turn out to satisfy us. We are full of frustration and conflicts. There could not possibly be the violence, the greed, the egoism we see in the world around us if our heads were not the slaves of our feelings. We are milling about shouting 'This is what we ought to do', 'That is the solution', crying, as in the Gospels, 'Lo here and lo there'! But the Kingdom of Heaven is within us.

And this Kingdom of Heaven is the domain of the essence, of the unalterable divine shape with which we were born, and which we ignore, not so much deliberately but simply be-cause we have forgotten it exists, because nobody ever told us about it.

But don't forget, this essential life in me, in you, in all of us, is only a possibility. It does not follow it will be realized. In fact by starving and squashing – and even killing – this sacred part, by living only in personality, we can destroy the only part of us that is worthy of faith and love and hope.

Daily life must be lived, yes. Daily struggle must be made, yes. But unless we set aside a time, every morning and every evening, when we try to shut out the world and its boisterous cacophony, and patiently, persistently search for and nourish this orphan, there can be no hope for us, such as we are.

So now! Shut out your noisy world. Be content only to follow your breathing and the quiet relaxation of your limbs. Sit in the heart of yourself, fighting for stillness, and if you do this day after day, you may certainly hope to reach that point of peace which is the eye of the hurricane. Believe me this is the deepest and most wonderful hope in life.

20

The Breath of Life

'If it does not sound true, pretend that it is true – and one day it will be.'

Have you ever thought what a curious thing breathing is? The air, our atmosphere, is a mystery. We know very little about it. Where does it come from? Not from the earth, obviously. Yet it is intimately concerned with our earthbound life. It penetrates everywhere. We depend on it, feed on it and take it absolutely for granted. Its sister water, which is almost equally ubiquitous, has a rhythm we can see, rising to mix with the air but falling to earth to complete its cycle. We can think of water as the blood of organic life, nourishing and sustaining all living things, but it is finite. We can accept the idea that there could be a certain fixed amount of water on earth which, though it gets trapped or held in suspension, slowly makes its way up to the skies and falls again with the sun acting as a sort of pump. Water, after all, is just a mixture of gases – oxygen and hydrogen – just like air!

But where does air come from? It too is a mixture of gases, varying with altitude and latitude, with light and darkness, and maybe with magnetic fields and solar wind. The earth's consumption of air is enormous, every breathing creature feeds on it. We humans could not live for three minutes without it. Millions of tons of oxygen are consumed daily – yet the consistency of the atmosphere never varies. What is used is immediately and everlastingly replaced! How? Where from? We take all this for granted. Air is given to us all free –

like life! Even when we poison it, pollute it, our atmosphere seems miraculously able to cleanse itself, digest all pollution in the vast sieve of space. But how?

I am no scientist, but it seems to me that our atmosphere must be re-created and constantly replenished and renewed by particles entering it from outer space, principally from the sun. By processes which we have not yet begun to unravel, our earth world is fed with exactly what it needs. As the space probes have proved already, other planets, at other stages of development, have quite different atmospheres, atmospheres in which life as we know it could not possibly exist. It seems as if some consciousness knew what its children – our sister and brother planets – need! Were the composition of our atmosphere to change, even slightly, all breathing life would expire in a matter of minutes. Life on earth is very delicately balanced.

All this started from asking questions about the air we breathe. But could the air have other qualities which affect our inner life? Many ancient teachings stress the importance of breathing and the benefits that can be received by those who consciously inhale it.

It is not a digression for me to bring in here an exciting aspect of the teaching of Gurdjieff because of his way of taking old ideas and giving them deeper understanding, new life. An example of this is the long-lost Law of Seven, one of the two primordial laws of the universe. We have quite forgotten its existence, just thinking of seven as a lucky number. But there are odd instances of the law lying about – the seven notes of the octave, the seven colours of the rainbow and even the seven days of the week – but its universal application remains quite unsuspected. Science has never heard of the Law of Seven.

It is basically a law of process, the seven steps by which things come to fruit. Air plays a vital part in one obvious instance of the working of the Law of Seven – the process of eating. We spend a good deal of time and energy thinking about food, preparing it and enjoying it, without having much idea of what happens to it after we have swallowed it. We understand it builds and maintains life and energy and most of us think of it as our only food, ignoring the other two – air and life impressions – both of which are continuously feeding us and are vital to our existence.

Our 'ordinary' food, on entering the mouth begins a seven-fold process of change and refinement. Along its digestive way it meets juices which separate the fine from the coarse ingredients in it. Part of it breaks down into waste which the body cannot use, other parts go to the strengthening of the organism itself; but a third part rises, step by step, continuously being refined, to make possible the highest function of which our bodies are capable – the reproduction of the species. The end product of our bodily food is the ovary of the female and the sperm of the male. This is its destiny. It comes from the earth, builds and maintains earthly creatures and finally makes possible the creation of more earthly creatures. But it has practically no part to play in what may be called our spiritual life, except in one particular.

The Law of Seven, this law of process, has one special characteristic. As it evolves it is dependent at one point on an impulse of quite another quality entering it from outside giving it a sort of shove which quickens the whole process and urges it forward. In the case of the food octave this extraneous urge is provided by air. Air is of quite a different quality, coming literally from heaven, and entering the refining process of ordinary food it, as it were, spiritualizes it and enables it to fulfil its sacred possibility – the creation of new life.

So what is the place of air in the growth of our spiritual life?

We all have a rough idea that we are two-natured. One part of us dreams of higher things, while the other is stuck in the mud. The air we breathe corresponds very well to this. Part of it is certainly essential food for our bodies; but another part, which we usually ignore, offers the possibilities and rewards of a different sort of life – and this is closely bound up with the conscious intake of air.

There is a still invulnerable place inside us we can call 'I' – not the ordinary egoistic 'I' we bandy about in practically every sentence we speak but something different, a sort of core or citadel. It is this 'I' that is fed by air. Every time we breathe in, we feed this 'I'.

When we breathe out it is different, something definite, an almost prosaic feeling of being alive, a 'that's that' feeling, all summed up in the word 'am'. 'I' breathes in; 'am' breathes out.

During the last year of Gurdjieff's life, he told many of those who came to see him in Paris: 'Say "I am." Say it often. Many times. Every day.'

This apparently simple exercise turns out to be terrifying. Try seriously to say 'I am' aloud or to yourself. Do the words ring true? They are, in themselves, the very essence of affirmation. 'Here. Now. I stand. I live. I am!' And yet, say it as we may, the words sound hollow, empty. They mean nothing. The truth is I am not. I am nothing.

The first time we glimpse the truth of this, we see what Gurdjieff called 'the terror of the situation'. In two words it strikes into the very heart of our lives and forces us to question the sense and aim of our existence. As repetition of the exercise makes it sink deeper and deeper into us, a sort of despair follows. If we cannot say this, the very root of our lives is hollow, empty. Nothing makes sense. There is nothing to hope for. Just shut the eyes and plod on . . .

It was not much later that Gurdjieff added his wonderful words of consolation. 'If it does not sound true, *pretend* that it is true – and one day it will be.'

We must continue to work, continue to pray, continue to hope.

Gurdjieff was not the first to utter these words of hope. In the eleventh chapter of St Mark you will also find them: 'Whatsoever things ye desire, when ye pray, believe that ye receive them – and ye shall have them.'

21

Possessions

There is everything in him – except himself.

We all have potential. Some of us have ambition. But whether you aspire to be a millionaire, a boxing champion or a prime minister, special talents and a determined dedication are required for the top jobs. Everything has to be sacrificed to the aim.

It is much the same in the spiritual life. It needs a super effort to become a saint. Given the call, given the vocation, a struggle has to be faced which grows more and more rigorous as it proceeds and only ends with death. To live by a set of values far above those of ordinary life costs a lot of effort. It is very expensive. That is why saints are rare.

But the rest of us who don't set our sights so high often have a true longing to live what we call a better life. It is intermittent. It comes and goes. But it persists. If the core of my life, the real me could somehow participate in my everyday living, I feel certain everything would be different for me. But somehow I can't bring the two things together. I don't know how, I need help. How to begin?

The first step is my decision. I need this. I must commit myself. I must jump into the water. Those who only put a toe in will never learn to swim. I start by trying to strip away all the imaginary wealth that has cluttered up my life over the years. I put myself in training, so to speak. I refuse myself the luxury of dreams. My problem, my aim, is really very simple; but it turns out I can't face simplicity. I find a million excuses not to come to the core of the matter.

And what is the core of the matter? The easiest thing: just to take a look at myself from time to time. No! You must be joking! What could be more pleasant? After all, can I deny I am the most fascinating, wonderful person I know? Who else?

Of course it does depend which side I look at. If I'm honest, I have to admit there's a shady side I tend to ignore. The truth is we all have a lot of people inside us and looking at all of them, pleasant or unpleasant, is part of our study – not judging, mind, not approving or disapproving: this is good, this is bad – just looking, just seeing: 'I am like that.'

But this isn't religion, you protest. It's just psychology. Right. All religion is sacred psychology. We ask for our sins to be forgiven. And what are our sins? They are our excesses. Too much anger, or envy, or jealousy or pride. We look for harmony, for inner peace. It is called a state of grace. And what is a state of grace? It is a state in which I accept myself as I am, as my conscience (which is the God within me) knows I am.

This is an enormous simplification. I look. I begin to see myself as I am. All sorts of things follow.

Plans, projects, criticisms, dreams of all kinds are my inner wealth, my most precious possession. I live in them. Parallel with these inner fantasies are the physical possessions that clutter up our exterior world. They show outwardly what we are inwardly. We can afford neither.

For we are all really mad about possessions. We can't have enough of them. We judge everything by what we can grab. How much has he got? If only I had half as much as he has! Our place in society, our self-esteem, our hopes, our objectives, all lie in material things. How we *live*, how we are – that is quite unimportant. What we *have* is all that matters.

But the truth is we have far too much of everything – at least some of us have. And we who have strain every nerve to infect the rest with this epidemic, this virus, this worldwide disease called 'more', which is sucking the life out of us. Making life easier makes us lazier, more dependent on gadgets and gimmicks which, we think, will make life more satisfying when in fact they only make it more boring and empty and dead. Crime, terror and violence are a direct result of boredom, of an empty life. The best recipe for law and order is hard work. But the trend is all the opposite – less and less for more and more; more and more possessions, more and more boredom, more and more frustration.

Down the ages, from Diogenes to Karl Marx, the world's wise men have all repeated the same thing: raising the standard of living lowers the standard of life, small is beautiful, less is more, simplicity and voluntary poverty far from constricting life are the only road to peace and happiness.

And, down the ages, the world has not paid the slightest attention. So, while we protest we are all for a better life, we never dream of ridding ourselves of the possessions – which stick to us like limpets. Needs we have and are entitled to; but 'want' is a monster whose appetite is never satisfied.

Has life grown richer or happier for all this clutter? We live on mortgages and overdrafts. The whole world is in debt. Our cares and frustrations grow with our gluttony for possessions. The first step towards a richer spiritual life is to get our priorities right in the worldly one.

The simple life thrives on vitality, courage, ingenuity and enjoyment. Maybe the overcrowding on our planet will drive us towards it. Out of evil, good can come. Meanwhile the slogan of all those who truly aspire after the Kingdom of Heaven might be not 'What do I want?' but 'What can I do without?'

What can I do without? That is the alternative to 'What do I want?' To opt out of our materialistic, plutocratic society, like Diogenes, is to be dubbed a blackleg, an eccentric, a crank. How to live better is the last thing the busy man is busied about. Yet it is the final question, the only question that is worth asking. Are we honestly satisfied with our lives? Are we living them? Or are the 1001 amenities we depend on for our 'happiness' living them for us? How much of my life springs from my own vitality? How much depends on the new car, the big blender, the giant TV and the latest electronic game? Take them away, how much would be left? And beyond all this, to what depths of stupidity have we sunk if we imagine that the senseless, endless demands for more can ever solve anything.

We are plundering the whole earth in our lust for possessions, slaughtering the whales, felling the forests, burning off the oil, to produce what? A way of life enforced by machine guns and bombs – and all the infrastructure of gimmicks and gadgets our so-called civilization produces to support them and what they stand for: greed and grab. Can we honestly look ourselves in the eye and say 'This is the good life'? It is leading us inexorably towards our own self-destruction.

It has been said that a man of honour puts more into any enterprise than he takes out. At this evaluation we are thieves and criminals second to none. What are we putting back into life compared with our endless exploitation of it? We call ourselves the lords of creation! Lords of destruction would be nearer the mark.

If we really were the lords of creation all our effort would be devoted to care and well-being, not only of our fellow men, but of the whole marvellous world of harmony and beauty that lies about us. We should think only of the future – how to leave life richer than we found it, how to serve the evolution processes for which we were created by God.

How many think like this? Most of us have our snouts so firmly jammed in the trough of materialism, it is doubtful if we can ever get it out. For that would mean renouncing everything we have been brought up to, everything we hold dear, and living a life devoted not to having but to being, that is a complete reversal of our personal lives towards simplicity, morality and benevolence, all far from the deathwish that haunts us today and all impossible unless the divine destiny of the life force – far above our petty humanity – prescribes it for us.

And if you think that these are just the ravings of a lunatic, remember Shaw: 'We need a few madmen about today. Look where the sane ones have landed us.'

22

Good and Evil

'The higher blends with the lower in order to produce the middle.'

I suppose it must have been as a boy in Bible classes that I first heard the phrase about Satan 'falling like lightning out of heaven'. It was so striking, such a way to accent in no uncertain terms that he really had been thrown out that I never questioned why he had been exiled, nor where he had fallen; presumably on earth or in the regions below it where he still lurked to work his wicked ways.

It wasn't until many years later when I came across the phrase again that I began to question what it could really mean. After all, I said to myself, Satan was exiled from heaven, which is the abode of God, so he must have been a member of the heavenly community. Judas, betraying the Almighty? If, as it is generally assumed, he represents evil, did God regard the earth as a sort of dustbin where you got rid of what you didn't want? It seemed a bit unfair. Why should we be corrupted and led into sin just because God didn't want to have such an influence around? That isn't the way a loving father behaves. It didn't make sense.

'And I saw Satan falling like lightning out of heaven.' Is it possible that in that one striking phrase we are being shown something fundamental about the nature of life itself? What is good? What is evil?

Gurdjieff tells us that one of the two primordial sacred laws of the universe is the Law of Three. It states that all events on whatever scale, from the creation of a galaxy to the formation of a snowflake, are the result of the coming together of three forces, one active, one passive, one reconciling: plus, minus, equals. This law has come down to us in the form of the Holy Trinity. We accept its central mystical quality without, perhaps, fully understanding that it is sacred because it creates every event in life. Nothing happens without the Law of Three. It is God's thumb-print on the universe.

So, if God and Satan are two opposite forces, as they seem to be, what is the third, the reconciling force which, as it were, brings them together, makes them blend, harmonize with each other? Gurdjieff actually defines the working of the law more clearly. He says: 'The higher blends with the lower in order to produce the middle.' So, in this case, good blends with evil in order to produce what?

Whatever it is, this must surely be the most all-embracing example of the working of the Law of Three. There is only one thing of comparable scale — life itself!

God blends with Satan in order to produce life!

Can that be true? Can all life be reduced to such a formula? Well, if it can, we must redefine the meaning of the words 'good' and 'evil'.

Good blends with evil in order to produce life.

I suppose that, as a generality, we might agree with that. It roughly represents the world around us. There are a million impulses of goodness, kindness, generosity, patience, forgiveness — and a million of egoism, greed, brutality, violence and murder. And the proportion in which these blend adds up to life as it is.

But the balance is very subjective. My good is not your good. My evil is not your evil. I am a freedom fighter; you call me a murderer. I have nothing and am out to grab all I can; you have everything and are determined to defend it. So it goes.

None of this is done in the name of evil. Everything is done in the name of good. So now good and evil are beginning to look different. Apart from a few psychopaths, diseased mavericks, who are mercifully a tiny minority, dreadfully disturbed, we are all out to do good – our good, of course. Nothing wrong in that.

So, if all we want is a better world, our revolts and strivings are just aspirations, aspirations for the self which, alas, grow into revolutions for the world. This is surprising. What started out to be something evil is beginning to turn into something good that can be admired!

If half the world is fighting to change things and the other half is fighting not to, is evil another word for change? Change after all is just an attitude to life, not something to be destroyed, but just accepted in the evolution of man.

Although we have been told that everything is in constant motion, that life is a dance, we cannot get rid of the fixation that somewhere there is a perfect state, which must somehow be reached and permanently set up. But perfect things are dead. They are finished. They have no future. Perfection is the last thing we want. What would life be without struggle, without effort? We should all sit about with our feet up, snoring, longing for change. There can be, must be. Divine discontent for the world to come is an attitude, not a state. You can hold on to an attitude, you cannot hold on to a state.

All this seems to have got us into a bit of a muddle. Are there definite categories of right and wrong, good and evil? Or are we really talking about forces, complementary to life, necessary to it, integral with it? Do we begin to see the first glimmer of a larger idea, a basis on which the whole universe could be built?

The first thing we have to get hold of in this question of good and evil is that the Creator is always *outside* his creation. The painter paints a picture: he is not the picture itself.

Gurdjieff, in his great creation myth, explains how our endlessness, the uni-being Creator was forced to bring the world into existence in order to combat the destruction of everything by time which would eventually threaten even the abode of His most glorious being itself. Whereupon He had the divine idea of setting up a self-recreating and self-maintaining world in which everything would depend on everything else, feed on everything else and thus, by continually renewing itself, defeat the endless appetite of time.

At the very heart of this creation lies the Holy Trinity, the manifested unity, three in one, of the living world from which the wheel of life is generated. First the positive creative force radiating outwards, downwards; then the denying force, constantly holding life in check by dissatisfaction with things as they are, striving upwards; and between the two, the eternal heartbeat in and out, down and up, a balance, always striving – such is our longing for perfection beyond this life – for some ultimate condition of peace, rest and calm, finally freed from the everlasting struggle to which life condemns us.

We live in a triadic universe where nothing can move or develop unless three forces are present. But largely because of the ignorance of those who are supposed to teach us, we have never been told about it and so remain ignorant, imprisoned in a dualistic world of right and wrong, black and white, yes and no. We are third-force blind and cannot see reality – and this in spite of having before our eyes every day innumerable examples of the Law of Three: flour, water and fire makes bread; father, mother and children make family; print, ink and paper make books; and so on, endlessly. Yet we obstinately drag on in our duality dungeons of hot and cold, big and small, sweet and bitter and are surprised, mystified and even furious when our lopsided prophecies fail to match what turns up.

So this one phrase from the Bible – 'And I saw Satan falling, like lightning out of heaven' – has led us into new ways of thinking about the creation and the Holy Trinity lying at the heart of it. Everything is connected, everything depends on everything else, all descends from the one. Satan is God's creation, as much worthy of praise and love as all the angels and archangels. They are all, to be prosaic, sitting on the executive committee of the creation.

But to end on a question: when God threw Satan out of heaven, was he throwing out time – his enemy, the universal destroyer, who was destined to oblige him to re-create the world continually and so make everything new?

23

Miracles

'To have faith whether consciously or unconsciously is for every man very necessary and desirable. Faith alone brings the intensity necessary for self-consciousness.'

What is a miracle – a divine manifestation of grace, a supernatural event, an answer to prayer, an amazing coincidence or just something we can't explain?

What is common to all these is a feeling that higher powers do sometimes act at a lower level. In general, we are very wary of such powers. We do not like things we cannot understand and go to a good deal of trouble to debunk them if we can by dismissing them as tricks, frauds or hallucinations; anything to keep life on an ordinary level we can control.

It was not always so. Ancient peoples took miracles in their stride. They evidently didn't feel so distrustful of the Almighty and so we get gorgeous miracles like the parting of the waters to let the Israelites escape from Egypt, or the trumpets that blew down the walls of Jericho, or Jonah being swallowed and later regurgitated by a whale. All these belong to an age when the Creator was thought to take a very personal interest in what was going on in this world and interfered with normal happenings in a quite arbitrary manner, playing games with the laws of the earth. Today we look on all this as great fun. We don't believe a word of it and think of it simply as a highly coloured way to romanticize the legends of the remote past.

It isn't really till we come to the Gospels that we begin to take miracles seriously. Some people find the miracles performed by Jesus Christ very disturbing because they seem to have nothing to do with the teaching. Bernard Shaw, for instance, found them irrelevant. It was ridiculous to say, in effect, 'You should love your enemies and to prove it to you I will now proceed to cure this gentleman of cataract.' But miracles are not to be so lightly laughed off. In fact it seems there are different orders of miracles.

First there are the legendary wonders of the virgin birth, the transfiguration and the resurrection. These transcend all the laws of life on earth and beget feelings of mystery, worship and awe for the person of Jesus himself. They are a sort of supernatural setting to the jewel of the teaching and lift all our thoughts and longings and hopes to a higher level because of the divine and tragic life from which it sprang.

Of quite a different order are what may be called the healing miracles. The whole life of Jesus is studded with innumerable acts of compassion and love which flowed from him in such a way as to 'make people whole' from all manner of physical and spiritual diseases. The laying on of hands is not an unknown art. Some people are given such powers and use them for the healing of their fellow men. But clearly Jesus disposed of these gifts to a degree far beyond anything recorded before or since.

But there is a third order of miracles which may be called the teaching miracles.

The wonder of miracles is the way they teach us there are higher levels of life and higher powers which enable certain people to show us that our understanding is to be found by those who search for something beyond the surface levels of belief.

But there is one great stumbling block in ancient writings which the modern reader does not take into account. Sacred writings of all ages – and there are even modern examples – have one thing in common: they are often couched in allegorical language, that is they mean more than they say – take them literally only and you miss much of what they can tell you.

Now this goes absolutely against our grain. Words nowadays are essentially pragmatic. They mean what they say. Life is serious and complicated. To keep us with it at all, we must have everything explained in clear simple language that a child can understand. In fact our vocabulary is shrinking to less than basic English and will soon be reduced to the computer jargon of the comic strip. We are forgetting how to handle words and the idea that there may be hidden meanings beneath the words is dismissed as esoteric nonsense. We have no time for it.

A lot of Jesus's teaching was given in parables, simple stories that had another meaning easy for anybody to understand. To make it clearer Jesus even explained some of his parables to get people into that way of thinking. If we have the wit to follow up these hints into the meaning of the parables, we can find layers and layers of meaning which, with contemplation, spread out into a web of understanding until we read, perhaps, quite a different idea of the sense and aim of our existence and begin to see the summons that is presented to us.

This, incidentally, is why we tamper at our peril with the older versions of the Gospels. They were written by people who understood the power and the upper harmonies of words. What we dismiss as archaic phrasing can be the key to the door of understanding that simplification locks shut.

The wonder of the Gospels is that there is something for everybody. The simpler parables lead on to those that repay more study, such as the wise and foolish virgins, the tares and the wheat and the prodigal son. But woven into what may be called the narrative of the teaching are other stories so cunningly contrived and ingeniously presented that we don't immediately see what we are being taught. The paralysed man who could not get down quickly enough to the well when the water was troubled, the unclean spirit Jesus met in the land of the Gadarenes, the vision of Satan falling like lightning out of heaven, all these are subtle and profound allegories of the life of man and the universe.

And now, at last, to the teaching miracles.

What may be called the teaching miracles are those stories in the Gospels which could not have ended as they did without the help of divine powers. The wedding feast at Cana when Jesus changed water into wine, the raising of Lazarus, the feeding of the five thousand, all these defy ordinary explanations and have become part of the legendary supernatural powers of our Lord.

But suppose we refer back to those ideas about language I mentioned before. Suppose here too there are deeper meanings below the literal tales? Let us take one such miracle, the feeding of the multitude.

To begin with, we have to make a jump, leaving below the literal meaning, and realize that the food that great numbers of people had come to partake of was not a meal for their stomachs, but for their spirit. Their need for this spiritual food was so great it made them flock to Jesus and his disciples. They were starved, just as many people today are starved and hunt everywhere to be fed.

When truly spiritual teachers are faced with congregations that 'hunger and thirst after righteousness' they are forced to examine themselves and, in humility, recognize they are inadequate to the task. A young French teacher, who died in 1944, put it this way:

I am dead because I have no wish.
I have no wish because I imagine that I already have one.
Imagining that I have one, I try to pass it on.
Trying to pass it on I see that I have nothing.
Seeing that I have nothing,
I see that I am nothing.
Seeing that I am nothing, I desire to become something.
Desiring to become something, I begin to live.

So it may well have seemed to Jesus and his disciples on that faraway day that they had so little to offer – five loaves and two small fishes. But it was eleven they had – and lo and behold, when they offered it, the food was so fresh and wholesome and nourishing that not only were they fed but, when the feast was over, 'they picked up the pieces twelve baskets full'.

Here perhaps is a deeper meaning in this parable. How many services have we attended? How many preachers have we listened to? How many broadcasts have we heard?

How much have we eaten?

Most of it we didn't hear, didn't interest us, or was forgotten. The good food remained uneaten and was left to be picked up by the teacher – twelve baskets full!

Perhaps the miracle is not the feeding of the five thousand, but the infinite patience and love of those who, despite the waste at the feast, stoop to pick up what is left and start all over again.

24

Contemplation

'Show me the elephant the blind man has seen and only then will I believe you have really seen a fly.'

'The way of contemplation' – the phrase has a comforting, almost soothing, ring to it. There's something attractive in the idea of settling down to have a good think about things. We feel that if we could really concentrate we could find a way out of all our difficulties and solve all our problems. And when it comes to more serious matters – well, the only way to come close to them to find out what we truly need to understand is by way of contemplation.

I don't know how it is with you but I find in those moments I set aside to contemplate things that are important almost immediately I come up against an unexpected difficulty. I find I really can't do it. Thinking deeply about a subject, concentrating on it, contemplating it, eludes me. I do wish to understand, say, why I am so impatient or quick-tempered or lazy or critical; and hardly have I put the question to myself than I find I'm off on all sorts of tangents thinking about totally irrelevant things, miles away from the point. Thoughts keep popping up like bubbles from a glass of soda water, burst and fizz all over the place; and if I'm honest I soon have to face the fact that I cannot stop it. I cannot control my attention.

So then what happens? Either I give it up and decide I'm not in the mood and I'll try again tomorrow when I'm quieter, or else I begin to contemplate not the subject itself but why I can't contemplate it. Why can't I keep my eye on the ball?

And the discovery of my inability to do what appears to be a perfectly simple thing ends by being very frustrating, very humbling; for the first time perhaps I begin to see myself. Thinking is a very mysterious process and what usually passes for thought is no more than a train of association. Random bits of experience are assembled from memory by the marvellous computers we all carry about with us; and thoughts seem to nudge one another along, just like buffers in a shunting goods train – one association prodding the next. Sometimes we can work back and see how we started out thinking about, say, our relations with some neighbour and ended up stuck at the forgotten name of a shop down the road.

Seeing that association is not thought is a much bigger step in understanding ourselves than we realize at first. It is the door through which we can enter that unknown world which bristles with awkward questions: What am I? What is my aim in life? To what end is it all leading me? Is there any sense in it? Or is it just a tale told by an idiot signifying nothing? There are lots of answers to these questions in books but the only ones that are really worth anything are those we come to by ourselves, by way of contemplation.

We are ready to admit that contemplation may be a very good thing, but such as we are we really cannot do it. At the same time a number of wise men have extolled its virtues as a spiritual method so how can we learn to do it? My dictionary defines contemplation as 'to think deeply' but what generally passes for thought is mere associative reaction, a reflex that is thrown up to the surface of our consciousness by everything that happens. We live by these reflexes, drawn from the memories in our computers. They are not *our* thoughts but things we have picked up second hand from a book, or a newspaper, or the television or whatever. But we have acquired a very clever trick. We can string them together in a new way and then they seem quite original and we pass them off as our own. Some people live their whole lives on these borrowed opinions and pretend to be intelligent people. But thoughts are something quite different. They do not originate in the fantastic card index we all carry about in our heads. Thought is something special and such as we are, we cannot command it at will.

We can think of ourselves as a house. We live on the ground floor – that is the office of our lives. But in the basement is a positive catacomb of stored memories, for every single thing we think or feel is recorded.

For everything we can remember there are ten thousand things we forget. But even so when somebody calls and presses the right buttons we can usually react by fishing up enough memories to keep the conversation going. But we also have an upper floor in the house and here our thoughts can be found. And the real problem about thinking is how to get upstairs, for the staircase isn't easy to find. By moments we do all manage to do it but *we can't do it when we want to.* We pop up there at most unexpected and apparently irrelevant moments. We all have the experience of being really troubled about some problem. We bring up all our reactions and associations and the answers don't seem right; they won't work, they're not what we want. We have to leave it, we cannot solve the problem. Then later, perhaps a day, a week, or even a month later we're cleaning our teeth or opening the garage door and there, suddenly, out of a blue sky when we weren't thinking about it at all there's the answer, full-blown, complete – without any worry, without any effort. It's a sort of miracle, very extraordinary, nothing to do with association. We call it 'inspiration' but it is really only the upper storey of our heads, our real thought working. Contemplation is reaching the upper storey more often, even whenever we want. But how?

So now if we've reached the point of finding out what contemplation is and a sort of inkling of the way it sometimes arises in us, unexpectedly, we might try to find some way of making it less haphazard, more available. Paradoxically it seems that to think deeply, to contemplate, we have to give up all ideas of thinking. This sounds ridiculous because these days we've become so used to thousands of voices shouting their so-called thoughts at us day and night, the very idea that there could be any communication without thinking doesn't make sense. What other way of communication is there?

Silence. Most people find silence awful, awkward, embarrassing, boring, a waste of time. We're all terrified of silence because then there's nothing to react to, nothing to chatter with and a frightening suspicion begins to arise in this nothingness of silence that we really are nothing, have nothing of our own, nothing to give – no meaning, no place. We rush into any sort of noise, any sort of chatter, to forget, to blot out our own emptiness, our own nothingness. But the way of contemplation is reached through silence and silence itself is not easy to obtain for it comes through discipline, through discipline in reaching for quietness, in calming and relaxing the limbs of the body, in filling the mind with nothing beyond the self, in sitting as it were inside a sphere beyond which my thoughts may not go.

Keeping all the attention within this sphere, within this self, a gradual quietness begins to brood in the heart which shuts off the railing of thoughts and feelings and fears and anxieties. A thousand times we escape out of it, and the world and all its chatter comes shouting back. But as often as it comes we reject it, cut it off, mend the rent in our shield and fight to repair the damage by a return to stillness and peace. This inner stillness has to be fought for and will not always come. But when it comes, far from cutting us off from life, it brings a new level of awareness more vital, more intense, more alive than anything we could find outside it.

The way of contemplation is not for everyone. It is very difficult in a busy life to cut everything off and retire into quietness. But for those who know the benefit from perhaps a gift of some chance experience, there is one thing essential and very useful. It is simply to try to form a daily habit, like brushing the teeth or combing the hair, of making room every day for a time in which to practise this search for silence. This, persevered with, can become a habit whose benefits will not disappear once they have arisen. Then we bless the day we began to bring such a wealth of comfort and fulfilment into our lives – and all by the way of contemplation.

25

Crisis

Two hundred conscious men could save the world.

W e don't know what to do. That, it seems to me, is the inevitable conclusion forced on anyone who tries to make sense of the problems in the world around him. We simply do not know what to do. We are looking everywhere for solutions and there seem to be no solutions – only an aggressive determination to disagree with every proposal, to block every agreement, to fight every issue and bring all national and international negotiations to a standstill. The whole world is living beyond its means. Everybody is in debt to everybody else and when it gets too tricky we just dishonour our debts and print new money. It is a worldwide phenomenon and, I repeat, nobody, but nobody, knows what to do.

If we are to find a way to avoid the global destruction at our elbow, we have to understand more clearly the way the world is put together. Every event in the universe, from the creation of a galaxy to the miracle of a snowflake, takes place under the action of three forces, under what is called the Law of Three. Science has never heard of this law. Religion knows it under the title of the Holy Trinity. It is one of the primordial sacred laws of the universe and it states that every happening, every event, consists of the coming together of three forces, an active force, a passive force and a neutralizing force, or, if you like, affirming, denying and reconciling forces, or simply plus, minus, equals.

We think we live in a dualistic world, right or wrong, either or, hot or cold, black and white; but there is always a third component. If we stop to consider for a moment we can easily see it. Flour and water will not make bread without fire, the growth of a plant requires light, moisture and earth. Chemists can give you many examples of processes that cannot proceed without a catalyst. But we have been conditioned to ignore this. We are third-force blind.

Until the third force appears the event cannot take place. A blow cannot be struck till my hand takes up the hammer. Bearings will seize up without oil. At best two forces stagnate or circle round each other, or they wither away.

The Law of Three is part of the nature of reality and failing to recognize it leads us continually into endless dualisms which can never solve anything. There must be a reconciling force, a neutralizing or comforting force, in effect a sort of compromise, which will resolve the situation or allow it to move forward.

If we apply this universal law to the conditions prevailing in the world today it is obvious that our approach to all problems is dualistic. We press harder and harder on the two sides, each determined to 'beat' the other. The rioters grow more violent and the police more determined. Mob hysteria provokes brutal reaction.

The list of these confrontations is endless. The posturing of the great powers, the haves and have-nots, Catholic versus Protestant, black versus white, the two sides stand embattled, neither will give way. But however much they may stand on their rights, there can be no solutions until the third force – often in some quite unexpected form – is allowed to enter.

There is certainly a third force at work in the world today which looks in another direction for a solution to all our problems. I refer to the upsurge of religious longing which manifests itself worldwide in all manner of cults, sects and original teachings. Subconsciously people know that things are far from right. They are searching; but they are often credulous and naïve, easily hoodwinked by spurious 'teachers' out for power or money. Nevertheless the impulse is there, though it is at present too vague, too disorganized, too scattered to have much weight. The workaday world disregards all this as eccentric, slightly potty and of no consequence. They may be wrong.

Established religions, sticking to their old dogmas and rituals, can do little to help out because their message is somehow empty, threadbare. Revitalization of the churches can only come from a deeper understanding of how to apply eternal truths to the modern world. On the other hand those who experiment with yoga or meditation, divorcing them from their religious roots, for purely selfish reasons, soon get tired of them and give them up. All this leaves those who dabble in it more lost, more disillusioned than before. You have to be persistent, lucky – and dedicated – if you really wish to help yourself by helping your fellow men.

I do not want to sound too portentous and solemn about this; but to introduce a third force capable of modifying the way things are going in the world today is hardly a holiday task. We are too far down the slippery slope. Something coming from a different source, a different level, is needed. This is unlikely to be a mass movement. More probably it will come – and it must come – from a small, highly concentrated, selfless group of people who, by the very quality of their lives, their devout acts to those around them and the resurrection of the values that they spread will subtly and mysteriously begin to set fire to such a wave of hope for a more honourable way of life that it burns the hearts of men. Outer power is nothing; inner strength is invincible. The force of an idea can change the world.

Even to dream of saving us all from our own pride and stupidity is herculean; but it is not impossible if enough people begin to wake up to their situation and resolve to quieten and purify themselves.

As a group of men planning an escape from prison co-operate in the digging of a tunnel and rejoice if only a few get away, so all those who come to serious work come not for themselves alone, but to serve an aim which they have set themselves as sacred.

To have such a sense and aim to our existence, to long for

the opening of conscience in our lives, is a call urgently presented to all serious men and women. To follow it truly is a trust to be zealously guarded.

Gurdjieff said: 'Two hundred conscious men could save the world.'

26

Prayer for the Day

'To possess the right to the name Man one must first be one.'

So, here is the day coming again. And I have to go out into it. I do not know what will happen to me. Maybe I have to face something unpleasant, maybe I shall meet an old friend, maybe I shall have an accident, make a mistake or have a surprise. Maybe this is my last day on earth. I do not know. The day that is coming is a mystery. Every morning I go out into undiscovered country, and I go out into it alone. However many friends I have around me, however much support upholds me, my acts are mine. Nobody can act for me. I am my own responsibility. I cannot escape it.

Sometimes we feel this and it frightens us. Much of our nervousness and worry, our headaches, our breakdowns, come from this inner fear because we do not know how to deal with life. And yet we have to deal with it. We are forced into action. It is as if we were put on trial every day – on trial for our lives. And, by the time the night comes and the chapter of the day is closed, there is a sort of reckoning. You can cast it up before going to sleep if you like: what have I done today that was good, what have I done today that was bad and what have I learned today. And this sort of self-confessional has healing in it because, by doing it, I face myself. However the day has been – good, bad or indifferent – I have lived it. There it is. Nothing can alter it.

Now this is your situation, my situation, everybody's situa-

116

tion and the question arises: if there is this mystery, this jungle of the unknown facing me every day and if I have to go out into it, what are my weapons? How can I defend myself? How can I bear myself honourably whatever my situation? That is the crux of the matter. How can I *be* towards life?

You remember Kipling: 'If you can meet with triumph and disaster and treat those two impostors just the same'. Well, it sounds fine and we imagine that somehow we ought to be able to feel like that, act like that; but the truth is we can't. We cannot, such as we are, meet the vagaries of life, the impostor, and treat everything as if it was equally important or unimportant. That is our problem.

We are subjective people. By that I mean we have our likes and dislikes, our desires and non-desires – or so it seems. But curiously, if you watch you may notice that there is always something behind the like and dislike, the want and don't want, which doesn't quite agree, which isn't quite caught up in it, a sort of observer, a referee, who isn't part of the game.

Finding the referee is really the problem. I am always taking sides. I am always in contradiction. I need someone to blow the whistle, stop the game and let me start again.

Help me to withdraw, O God, from the jungle of life and find Thee in quietness.

So, here is the day coming again and wherever you are – already out on the road driving, or lying in bed thinking about your problems, or eating your breakfast and waiting for the news – it is 10,000 to 1 that you're in the same situation as everybody else, that is, faced with some sort of problem, some sort of contradiction, which you can't solve and which – again it's 10,000 to 1 – you'll leave to solve itself as we say, or leave it to chance, to the spur of the moment.

But even if you do leave it to solve itself, your *way* of meeting every situation is yours, something special, not quite the same, indeed possibly quite contradictory to the way your neighbour would meet it. We all have our own yardstick by which to measure the values in our lives. The trouble is we don't stay the same. Our tape measure is elastic. We fluctuate. We are full out for something one moment and have gone cold on it the next. We constantly contradict ourselves.

Now this is a curse – and it is also a blessing. For if we fall pretty low, it's certain, by the law of averages, that an hour or two later we shall rise pretty high. If we could learn to control these fluctuations, put a damper on the swings, everything would be a good deal simpler for us. Only children spend time on seesaws.

So the question is, how? And the answer is, it's impossible to learn this sort of life control in twelve easy lessons. It isn't that it's difficult. What we have to learn is perfectly simple; but we are so constructed that, such as we are, we can't.

Now, before we come to what it is and why we can't do it, I think we ought to be clear about one thing. In the spiritual life as in daily life, you have to pay for things. You can't have something for nothing. We've rather got into the habit these days of thinking a lot ought to be done for us. We almost feel that God owes us a harp and a pair of wings if we don't do anything criminal.

It is said that the Kingdom of Heaven is a pearl of great price. Have we got the money to pay for it, even on the never-never – for that is allowed? But the question is not really there. It is, 'Am I interested in pearls? *Do I really want it?*'

You remember how it is in the Sermon on the Mount: 'Blessed are they which do hunger and thirst after righteousness, for they shall be filled.' Hunger and thirst are the operative words in that Beatitude. Do we really want what we protest we want so much?

It's an absolutely basic question and everything depends upon it. And, to be truthful, we can't answer it. Why? Because of our seesaw, because of our fluctuations. At one moment salvation is the only thing that matters, at the next it's totally irrelevant. That is how it is. We have to be honest with ourselves. That's how it is.

Lord, help me to answer honestly, what do I want – *now*?

So, here is the day coming again, the first day of the rest of my life, and I suppose if you're reading seriously, it's because you are looking for help, for some signpost that will enable you to direct your life more profitably. We writers can only point and say, if you follow up this or that idea it may be useful. Whether it is or not depends on you.

So the first thing is to get out your spiritual mirror and take a look at yourself, to ask: 'Do I really want to change, to be better?' Well, yes and no. Sometimes I do, sometimes I don't think about it. But, sooner or later, we must come to a decision. And if the decision is to struggle to understand ourselves and our lives better, we must stick to it, come hell or high water. Otherwise we go round in circles.

What does it amount to? It can be put in many ways. Suppose we say that we feel, somewhere deep within us, an instinctive need to find the marvellous core that is already within us, and never to lose touch with it.

To hell with our sins, our shortcomings, our failures! We all have them. What I am determined to do, more and more, every day, is to come back, to come back again and again, to that certainty that there is a place that nobody can get to but me, that is absolutely, personally, mine.

But the trouble is I forget.

Maybe I truly believe that the Kingdom of God is within me, could I but find it. Maybe I know that if I could really see myself, I should see God. You remember Job: 'Though worms destroy this body, yet *in my flesh* have I seen God.'

We know this, feel it. That was why we committed ourselves in the first place – and what does our struggle turn out to be? Simply not to forget our wish to be present to our life.

Maybe you don't quite understand what I mean. Let me make it clearer. Whatever we are doing at this moment, we don't really know we're doing it. Life goes on by itself in us. How are you sitting now? Where are your hands? How are your feet placed? *Now*, I know. In a moment I shall forget. But we must try, desperately, to come back, again and again, first to the sense of our bodies, later to the whole of us. You think this is strange? But how can you expect to find the altar before you know the temple in which it stands? The first step towards the Kingdom of Heaven within us is through this body in which it dwells.

Lord, have mercy on my forgetfulness. Help me to remember my self. Amen.

27

Choice, Morality, Conscience

'. . . Objective Conscience is not yet atrophied in them but remains in their presences almost in its primordial state.'

CHOICE

I wonder if you have the same difficulty as I have. I've reached the point that listening to the news or reading the paper leaves me absolutely flummoxed. I really don't know what to believe. In fact I begin to wonder if I can believe anything – or anybody! All day I am bombarded by people telling me what I ought to believe about this, that and the other thing. Everyone thinks he knows – and all the truths are different! And it isn't only personal. Whole countries, nations, are arguing, threatening, fighting for these truths. Nobody can give way. Nobody can agree. It's getting to be a sort of nightmare. A lot of intensely reasonable, persuasive people shaking their fists at one another, and nobody listening. It doesn't make sense.

I must say I find it all terribly frustrating. It puts me on the defensive. I find I'm beginning to be against things, against others, like everybody else. And I don't want to be against people. I want to agree with them. I feel I must find some place away from all this, a place where I can be safe, if you see what I mean, a place where all this won't bother me, where I can keep my sanity. I can't opt out of it. I have to go on living. I see that, but if only I could find a line to follow, some sort of rudder! If only I knew how to sort things out, how to discriminate between the rights and the wrongs, the truths and the lies, that would be a great help.

A rudder! That might be a clue: a way to steer, to choose. The idea surprises me; but after all, I can choose. I am doing it all the time. I prefer this to that. I decide a hundred times a day between all sorts of things, big and small, choosing is second nature to me. Then why not choose what to believe?

Choosing in ordinary day-to-day things is easy, almost automatic. I have certain preferences, tastes, inclinations, and I follow them; but when it comes to things I've no control over, when I'm only indirectly concerned, just taking a stand, holding an opinion, then it's much more tricky. In a way it doesn't matter. What difference does it make, believing this or that? Why not sweep it all under the carpet and forget it?

But every so often another part of me surfaces, a part that knows quite well that this God-given Power of Choice is a clue to living. It is something sacred, given to no other creatures on earth. It is there for me to use and to use in a certain way, a way that I have to find for myself, in obedience to something I can't quite define, but which seems to be there, like a sort of compass needle deep inside me. But what is it?

MORALITY

We have been talking about choice, about choosing between alternatives, this or that, yes or no. And I said it is possible to examine an idea, a point of view, a belief, and accept or reject it. So choice is a sort of tool, a knife I can insert into life to divide things, to sort out for myself what is right and what is wrong – or rather what seems to me to be right or wrong – at that moment.

Ah, that's the catch! I find my rights and wrongs are always changing, with the news or the weather or how I feel at the moment, with what I call my moods. What seemed essential at breakfast seems irrelevant at lunch, what I thought of my colleague yesterday is not what I think of him today, and so on and so on, endlessly. So to find something to stand up to these changes I must learn how to hold a course, have something to steer by. That's what I need – something to come back to, a line to help me find my way through all these changes that sweep through me.

I suppose the obvious line to turn to is what we call morality. Now morality is a very powerful word, with all sorts of overtones of social and religious behaviour. But curiously, it seems to me, in all our arguments and doubts and suggestions for cleaning up our increasingly permissive society, it is a word you hardly ever hear used. Nobody seems to measure our behaviour against the yardstick of morality.

I think this is because what the young call 'old-fashioned' morals are quite out of date. And it's true that many of them were simply sets of rules arising out of prejudice, class or fashion and are meaningless today. Today, for instance, we use the word immoral almost entirely in a sexual sense. We don't think of calling thieving or corruption or crime immoral. The word doesn't seem to fit. The idea behind it has lost its weight, its meaning.

So, to come back to our personal problems, if I hope to find help from morality, I have to ask myself what sort of morality. I have to go deeper. Maybe I have a sort of idea there could be another sort of morality, not swayed by day-to-day social changes, rooted in immemorial truths. But what is it? What are these truths it is based on?

Funnily enough, although I found answers in many different kinds of holy books, all that didn't give me any more than an impulse to reflect. And what I finally came up with was that real morality was something very personal, something which, for want of a better word, I call my conscience. But conscience is another of these odd, faintly disturbing words. What is my conscience really? How can I refer everything to it?

CONSCIENCE

So now we've picked our way through the bog of contradictions and misunderstandings of daily life to find morality.

And morality, when we examined it more closely, turned out to be conscience in disguise.

I don't know how it is with you, but the word 'conscience' always gives me a sort of guilty feeling. We say we have things 'on our conscience' or that we have done something 'with a clear conscience'.

And indeed, although we often use the word lightheartedly, it does have a certain sting to it, as if it touched some hidden core deep inside us. So maybe it's true. Maybe the word does carry a meaning, a truth, which touches us.

Gurdjieff calls conscience 'the representative of the Creator in us' and this at once focuses our thought for it suggests that God lives within each of us in the form of conscience and dwells there as the final arbiter in our lives, the final standard against which we can measure everything we are and do.

At the same time it faces us with the impossible, for how can we, such as we are, live the life of perfection His presence demands? Yet, whether we know it or not, the Kingdom of God is within us.

So we begin to marvel at the wonder and depth of the word 'conscience'. Our longing is not for something far away. It is within us, always there, could we but find it, and with it the compassion of the Master who, in accepting to live in such a house of clay, must know and accept its limitations, must know it is only a tenancy He has taken on, must know and forgive our shortcomings and imperfections.

There are those who do not know of His presence, do not even suspect it and have, so to speak, banned Him to the attic or the basement of their lives; but He is there all the same and to those who begin to know it, He offers a sort of rule of the road, a guide to daily life, our conscience.

It is not easy for, even when we have accepted the idea that we have a conscience it is difficult to find it. We are not looking for any worldly ready-made set of precepts or regulations, but the flash of truth which we know, when we find it, to come from another place. How to find that place?

Today we live in a world of violence, terror and sudden death under the imminent threat of self-destruction. Yet, at the same time, parallel with it and parrying it at every turn, we see a rising tide of revulsion at the folly, ignorance and stupidity of those who prefer death to life. In such a desperate struggle what can be the reconciling force to which we can turn for help? What else can it be but the infinite mercy of God, the cry of His conscience rising in each one of us.

28

Work in Progress

'Within the coarse body of a man there is a fine and invisible body which is just the soul.'

It has been said that the visible world is the organization of invisible vibrations. It seems the human destiny is to explore the visible and ruminate on the invisible. Determination to unravel and understand this insoluble puzzle is the preoccupation of creatures living on an insignificant planet called Earth, satellite to the centre of a minute solar system, whirling in a sea of stars. This earth has somehow acquired a protective and transforming veil called the atmosphere and beneath its shield a phenomenon called life has appeared. It is a sort of fungus, a very thin and delicate film, which has evolved on the surface of the Earth. It is referred to as organic life or Great Nature and man is an animal, part of it.

These three partners, as they may be called, Earth, atmosphere and Nature are beings, different in form and shape from human beings, but living entities, closely linked and known to man as life, 'his' world, in which he is almost wholly absorbed. At the same time he is aware of being related to other worlds above and below him, but the difference in scale is so vast it is almost impossible to realize the relation – zero to infinity.

How should he relate to the living cells of which he is composed and conceive of them as beings with an individual life, place and purpose, a cycle as real to them as his life is to him? Or how should he relate to Great Nature as a whole, as a single living being, with its sickness or health, its needs and desires, its growth and decay, its lifespan and destiny among suns and comets, as far beyond man as are his cells within him? And, as for the Earth, immeasurably beyond both man and Nature, what connection can it possibly have with this itching skin which has recently grown on its surface?

Yet these three beings, living in utterly different time scales, each part of totally different worlds, are yet all inevitably interdependent, interrelated, co-existent, one. This is the miracle, the enigma of the whole.

If man tries to make an approach to this mystery of which he is a part, it seems the limit of his understanding is an assumption that there is, somewhere beyond his knowing, a force which, in a moment of incandescent ecstasy, caused our universe to be created.

The first act of this uni-being Originator was to bring to life a creation made in His image, to give form to the eternal in the substance of the temporal. Then, out of His omniscience, love and desire for its increase and enrichment, He so ordered it that there should be, beneath His sovereignty, princes, suns, charged with the duty of carrying out his will. The families that grew up around these suns came to be called systems, solar systems, and these, in their turn, emanating their love for him, inspired everything around them to grow to similar patterns. And so it came about that, from the highest to the lowest, suns inspiring satellite suns, the wheels within wheels of the whole creation became saturated with a single impulse, the worship of the Lord God, whose Holy Spirit created and held all together in an everlasting and divine unity.

While the uni-being Creator remained hidden beneath His creation, his suns shone throughout his universe in a brilliant exuberance, reflecting his glory, each, whatever its place or dominion, the direct inheritor of the source, each seen by its family of satellites as the presence of God in its midst, each receiving from it everything necessary to its needs.

So, on man's little Earth everything originates and flows

from its sun. Without it no life can be created or multiply, die
or be born. But the life is unique to this Earth on which it
grows. It is created and confined within its atmosphere.
Beyond it no life, as it is known to man, exists. Outer space is
dark, cold and empty. It is the atmosphere which filters and
transforms the emanations of the sun into categories we can
recognize and separate, though they are no more than com-
ponents of the whole which is God, life itself.

This life on earth has existed and developed for millions of
years before man appeared on the scene. Great Nature has its
own life, its aims and needs and urges for self-development,
and does not exist, as man seems often to assume, exclusively
for human pleasure and profit. Indeed viewed impartially,
our 'world' may be only a temporary, transient phenomenon.
A few degrees' change of temperature, up or down, would
result in it being fried, frozen and forgotten, like a poor
season before the next spring.

Meanwhile, over a few million years, time has watched the
evolution of Great Nature, organic life on Earth, a marvellous being of such complexity, such infinite, inexhaustible
profusion and beauty that its perfection is evidently divine,
far beyond any understanding possible at the mortal level.

Every creature, part of this whole, has its own nature, its
own place, and strives only to perfect itself within those limits
to maintain the balance of the whole. But man stands in a
unique relationship to all this. While he is inextricably part of
it, must eat and be eaten like every other living thing, he has
been endowed with a curious faculty not developed elsewhere
in Nature: his mind, his intelligence. This challenges him to
explore beyond his own, instinctive human pattern and to see
– dimly and in part only – himself and the universal life
around him.

Within his search for a deeper understanding of those powers
which control the unfolding of his destiny, there remains,
woven into the weft of it, man's search for his individual
place in the pattern of it all. Where does he stand, what are

his links with powers so clearly above and beyond him? What is the purpose of his life? Why this wish for perfection, this longing to usurp the role of God, to find some reassurance that he is not doomed to oblivion?

This call for some answer, some comfort, some compassion from the godhead, varies from man to man. Some have no sense of it, nor interest in it, nor wish to think of it at all. Others feel there is 'something' there, but it is a mystery too deep for their understanding, and they remain content to worship it and wander in the maze of legendary euphoria in which it abounds. But there are a few in whom a secret urge manifests itself from time to time, haunting them, calling them towards another self – part dream, part longing, part faith, part hope – a sacred mystery, central to life, temporal yet immortal. It is the call of what we call the soul, the essence of our mortal nature, capable of surviving death, and although not clearly defined or understood, is held to be man's most precious possession, the sacred core of his life.

Some throw the net far wider. They say all living creatures have a soul. It is the point of contact between the temporal and the eternal, the terminal at which the life force enters, where God is made flesh.

Though all life is conceived and lives by the entry of this power, to some men alone has been given an instinctive wish to struggle to grow around it the seeds of everything that they sense as being holy in those strange, precious moments that come to them when they are possessed by a certain communion with the divine. This distillation of everything godlike a man has discovered, cherished and stored during his life becomes his true weight, his spiritual specific gravity, so to speak, the presence which makes him what he is.

So when the time comes for him to leave this vessel in which he has grown his soul, this love clings to the life force, the living God within him and rises with it towards the source. There, at the gates of our world, the limits of our atmosphere, a mystery, a miracle occurs. Still half mortal, unable long to live without a body, the abandoned soul, unable to rise higher, may meet and mix with another being of a like nature, join the descending stream of life and be reborn.

All earthly life carries within it the promise of another. Man, if he so wishes, can grow his soul, the mortal part his longings have made immortal. On the sum of such longings depends the evolution of mankind and therefore through it of all life on this earth. This is the nature of the promise of eternal life. It is God's will being done.

29

The Big Bang

'Don't they really ever see that these processes of theirs are the most terrible of all the horrors which can possibly exist in the whole universe?'

Do you remember the first time you read something about the Big Bang – that moment when the universe is said to have been created? I remember I just couldn't take it in. It was such an extraordinary idea – the whole universe an explosion! But, bit by bit I came round to it. Everything must have started somehow. That idea would do as well as any other.

The scientists, as far as I could make out, working backwards, had come to the conclusion that there had been a moment of universal explosion – an enormous bang! And they had calculated, millisecond by millisecond, what happened immediately after the bang. But what about the moment itself when, out of nothing, something so fantastic as the universe was created? Who pressed the switch? On that they were wisely silent.

All the same, since we live in a world which is, for us, governed by time, by there being a before and after, if we get involved in a question so ridiculously beyond us, we may as well ask it. Was there anything before the Bang, some force, some universal presence, utterly beyond our knowing? Down the ages there must have been wise men who pondered about these unanswerable questions, who conceived the idea of some great Originator who stood behind it all and could explain the why of the creation.

And of course there were such wise men and it didn't take long to find them. And their answers were perfectly clear.

'In the beginning was the Word. And the Word was with God and the Word was God.' The opening words of St John's Gospel have such magnificent authority they sweep us up into another world – a world without time. We can't understand it. But just to absorb it, to accept it, is enough. Later, saying the words over and over, a meaning begins to emerge. That beginning when nothing was to become something, before anything had been created, that 'Word', whatever it was, and is, was 'with' God, and 'was' God. It was His conception, still creating itself within him and the creation absorbed him completely, it *was* Him. It had not been given to the world we know – the temporal world. The creation had not taken place.

What was this 'Word'? Those four letters carry a wealth of promise, a sort of awe at all they could stand for. I carried them around with me for years, wondering ... For we who live in time can there be any beginning? On our little world there is certainly creation, but before creation there must be the idea, the impulse, the love. Could one dare transfer such an idea up to the very summit?

In the beginning came this moment of incandescent ecstasy – the Word! 'All things were made by Him and without Him was not anything made that was made.'

All things were made by Him – so the Bible says, But not all at once, surely? Not all complete, finished, perfect? He must have left us with some sort of hope, a challenge at every level, from which the creatures living at that level felt they could grow. Without that there could be nothing to live for, nothing to love. For, back of it all, we see a built-in urge for everything in God's creation to create, to grow towards perfection. Growth is the driving force that powers the universe. Everything, at its own level, strives to perfect itself at that level.

But while He, the eternal root of it all, remained hidden, his children – in the shape of suns – shone with white-hot exuberance and joy. Their task was to begin to spread and shape the everlasting renewal of life and love in the temporal world. These suns themselves were not identical, they were living individuals, 'full of grace and light', each destined to follow its own growth and display His glory in a different form.

So this first universal scattering of suns began to create its own order, swirling into galaxies, forming solar systems, each sun gathering children, planets, round itself to form a family with its own character and individual life.

We cannot really conceive of beings, living entities, on a scale higher than our own, nor of this giant stairway by which life descends in steps from life-giving suns to dark planets, from planets to their moons, from moons to the life lived upon them, nor from the life on one such planet, after ten million years, to human beings, part of that life, no more than dust at the bottom of it all.

Yet this dust, which we are, is still part of the whole, part of Nature, mother to a profusion of other living beings, all of which are given, according to their needs, the power to live and love. In such a manner is the whole universe saturated with adoration to that uni-being by whom it was created.

Moreover every particle of this self-renewing world constantly showers love on all about it, rejoicing to return it to God in the form of beauty. Beauty is the homage of life to its Creator.

This was the Golden Age, the time of the world's youth, when all was young and new, when the magic carpet of our life lay lightly on the surface of the earth and every creature lived by instinct. Life turned on food and mating. Body was all. It was a closed and simple circle, perfect, complete – until the chessboard of choice appeared. Then, slowly, all life became a question.

It had to come. There had to be a mind by which all life could see itself, a guardian intelligence, a crown to the creation. So God created man to watch over the growth of life on earth, to help advise and supervise a way by which it could move forward. Alas, some of these guardians, lacking ability and understanding, dared to usurp God's will and interfere, twisting his laws to suit their own lust for power and profit.

Then others, seeing disaster looming, cried out: 'This is an outrage against life! Let us get back to that harmony which already existed in our world until mankind defiled it.'

How are we to find our way back to this harmony which already existed everywhere on earth until we human beings came to defile it? Well, suppose we go back to the Bible: 'All things were made by Him and without Him was not anything made that was made.'

We have to take the words literally – there is nothing that is not created by God, in which His presence is not present. He is pervasive, intrusive into everything that exists. Do you think that the sun just provides us with heat and light? The sun is the active presence of God in our midst, the emanator of life itself, present from moment to moment in every life and every need, desire and hope for which His creation clamours. The final trinity on which the universe rests is God, life and love.

The very word 'creation' is enough to remind us that everything changes, must change, must constantly renew itself. With every creature born an inbuilt desire for growth is also born, and with that growth the will to multiply and with that the struggle to dominate.

What curbs the need to dominate? For after all there is a limit to what the earth can bear. What prevents it being overrun by the most aggressive, the most prolific species? It seems that in the beginning an order of divine justice was decreed in which the Creator set up a complex system of checks and balances. Every creature was guaranteed a living place, but the most ingenious and subtle disciplines were created which prevented it exceeding that place. From this there resulted an infinitely diverse but stable entity, a being we call Mother Earth, which having already existed for a few million years was not challenged until a new type of being appeared on the scene, just recently.

Great hopes were placed by the Creator on this newcomer. If His hopes were realized all life on earth could be refined and raised to a new level. And with this God forsaw infinite possibilities in the harmony of a conscience-loving world.

At first all went well. These beings, called people, prospered and multiplied. But later, alas, their intelligence – which was the unique gift God had bestowed on them – grew like a Jericho trumpet in crescendo until they imagined themselves to be masters of the world – and threatened all life on earth.

Then alarms began to sound throughout the solar system. Mother Earth warned them that they risked their own survival if they did not discipline themselves. But, blinded by vanity and greed, they ignored the call.

So Great Nature, to save herself and all her children from this epidemic of suicide, was forced to set in action powers of a higher order. Already her seas and skies were polluted. Drought, famine and useless wars had spawned deadly diseases. Incurable sicknesses spread worldwide. Whole peoples were collapsing. From greed and ignorance of Nature's basic rhythms a situation close to chaos had arisen. A new start had to be made. But a return to sanity and health would not be easy. Much would seem worse before it could grow better.

Nature's aim was to return man to his role of lord of the creation for which he had been created. But to do this he himself had to change. He had lost his manhood and his inner self and wasted his unique gift of intellect. His nobility of purpose and morality had sunk under a sewage of corruption. An all-round lowering of life standards to subhuman levels had bred low resistance to disease and dependence on every kind of medical or psychological 'cure' to save him from a state from which he had grown unable to save himself.

Such a crisis may well eliminate all those without stout hearts and the resistance to survive. Coupled with all-round interference with the laws and rhythms of Nature, drought, famine and other forms of self-destruction, huge falls in population may result. But those who come through are likely to have strains of a better quality of human life, having fought their way through this nemesis of shame and dishonour to rebuild our shattered world.

It remains for us to salute those who survive to guide us through this shadow of death to serve Great Nature in the world to come.

What is the price of forgiveness for our sins, O God?

Here. Now.

We were standing thigh deep in warm, still, sunlit water.
Along the shore a line of pink oleanders.
Behind, a small taverna where a peasant family served guests in summertime.
She lunged away, idly picked up a scrap of floating seafern, stood looking at it closely.
She had seen something.
Come! she called.
Half hidden in fernleaf lay three white sea flowers no bigger than sequins. They shone, bowed, nodded from their hair stalks.
She held them up for me to see.
And look, look!
The tiniest black beetle was climbing among them.

Out of the whole ocean, to find this!

We stood together. It was timeless.

Here He is!
Now!
Everywhere!
Always!
Ours!
His.

We stood for some time, looking.
She slid the miracle back into the sea.

Later we all lunched together under the trees.
The fish was delicious.
We talked a lot about the other world.
It was most interesting.